MW01630020

At Home

Alice Neel in the Queer World

At Home

Alice Neel in the Queer World

HILTON ALS

ALEX FIALHO
EVAN GARZA
WAYNE KOESTENBAUM

David Zwirner Books

HILTON ALS

INTRODUCTION

When I was a callow youth, I read—devoured, really—a book by Calvin Tomkins called *The Scene: Reports on Post-Modern Art.* Published in 1976, *The Scene* is comprised of profiles of art-world figures, Robert Rauschenberg and Robert Wilson among them, who came to post-abstract expressionist prominence working in a variety of media. Written in Tomkins's characteristically lucid, energetic style, *The Scene* pulsates with excitement, not only around his subjects, but about art's possibilities, and the ways in which the worlds of fashion, finance, and power converge.

Aside from opening doors and windows onto certain marquee names such as Nam June Paik, *The Scene* had the added benefit of introducing me to a couple of creators I had never heard of before, including the legendary printmaker Tatyana Grosman and Billy Klüver, who founded E.A.T. (Experiments in Art and Technology). But the pieces I was most drawn to in Tomkins's book focused on queer minds that, by virtue of their creativity, power, and access to one another, made me feel that the New York art world was, by and large, a queer one. And, if this was true, I thought, there might be a place for me in it.

I was not out to my family when I read *The Scene.* (My aunt outed me to my mother when I was nineteen.) And so I clung to those real-life gay people in books and magazines as then living examples of what was possible if I survived.

Tomkins wrote about Andy Warhol, of course, but the strongest queer profile, it seemed to me, was devoted to the life and times of the curator Henry Geldzahler. Born into a wealthy Jewish family in Antwerp in 1935 and educated at Yale and Harvard, Geldzahler was one of those preternaturally intelligent people that New York invites in by the boatload to keep feeding itself. From 1967 until 1978, Geldzahler was the curator of twentieth-century art at The Metropolitan Museum of Art. In addition to Warhol, with whom he spoke on an almost daily basis for years, Geldzahler was close friends with the British artist David Hockney, and to say I wasn't entranced by the gay circles Geldzahler frequented—and somehow opened up like a pebble tossed into a pool—would be a lie. I was fascinated by the queer ripple effect, by that pool of gay artists and women artists who contributed to the land and water of my imagination.

In the many paintings and photographs Geldzahler sat for throughout his career, one can see that he never really lost his baby fat, and he never lost his very unique way of looking at his contemporaries' work, which, for him, did not seem to include, at the time he curated his landmark 1969–1970 exhibition, *New York Painting and Sculpture: 1940–1970*, any work by Alice Neel.

In 1977, just before he officially left the Met, Geldzahler was appointed commissioner of cultural affairs by then Mayor Ed Koch, and the gay upon gay of it all cannot be ignored. Nor can the fact that Neel, one of the best recorders of life in her New York before and after the Second World War, through Vietnam and the start of the AIDS crisis, has outlasted all those who shut her out of the game, whether it was Geldzahler, as he was putting together *New York Painting and Sculpture*—art-world folks just called it

"Henry's show"—or any other aspect of the New York art world, where women have rarely if ever rated as well as men critically or financially. Of course, Neel's triumph is her work, and in looking at her *Henry Geldzahler* (1967; p. 46) I see several forces at work, including the artist's powerful ability to represent the thing—a person—as he or she or they are, as opposed to what she wished or they hoped they would be.

Most of us survive by drawing a curtain between ourselves and reality, but Neel pushed that curtain aside in order to tell the truth of her experience, and yours, in a single frame. The frame of experience. In *Henry Geldzahler*, the coddled, pudgy boy looks as though he's lately become a man, or at least a college student. We think he's completely in repose at first, but Neel doesn't let the painting go at that. His bespectacled eyes are not exactly focused on revealing what's in his soul; he could be looking over the viewer's shoulder—Neel's shoulder—to see who of greater importance might be entering the room. Then there is his left hand; the fingers curve upward, the valuable ring he wears is in direct contrast to his undergrad garments. What does Henry want? What does Alice want from Henry? I think it's fair to say that Neel, who was born in Pennsylvania in 1900 and who was, at the time she painted *Henry Geldzahler*, a nearly seventy-year-old woman who had worked in obscurity for most of her artistic life, wanted to be recognized by a powerful curator, which would mean inclusion in an art world where she then had no voice. But as she had done for most of her life, Neel made a place for herself out of no place, including the gay cultural world Geldzahler, Warhol, and others dominated at that time. And why not? For her entire professional life, she had worked against trends: she knew who she was. She knew, too, that the art world was defined by the rules of fashion and that she would make her time on this earth count by being redoubtably herself.

I think of the book you hold in your hands as a book of voices, all of whom are in dialogue with that singular voice—Alice Neel's. When she died in 1984, Neel had a great number of masterpieces to her credit, a galaxy of masterpieces, I would say, that bear witness to the terror we usually turn away from, having no language for it, namely alienation, disconnect, love. But these thoughts—feelings—have never been particularly easy to digest. As my student-self pored over Tomkins's profile of Geldzahler, I spent an equal amount of time with the catalogue for Neel's 1974 retrospective at the Whitney Museum of American Art, in part because by lifting the curtain between her subjects' constructed self and reality, Neel showed me my own curtain, my fears and shame about being gay.

As an artist, Neel gave so many people their name—the right to their name. So doing, she told us that no person is fixed; we have as many names as the lies we tell, the truths we live. In my dreams of a glittering gay world, as exemplified by Geldzahler, Warhol, and the like, it never occurred to me that that universe wasn't about inclusion; my imagination already included me. But Neel's paintings offered something definitive and real, something larger than "identity." She seemed to be saying in canvas after canvas that there was no word or image that could equal those fleeting moments of joy—of connectedness—that bound her not only to her subjects, but to painting itself, that solitary act that she performed in front of other people.

Sometimes in the silence of the paintings you wonder what was said during a Neel session, what language Alice used as she and her subject talked about the old times, the new times, and probably everything in between—same-sex love and domestic harmony or discord mixed in with bitchy jokes and empathy—given that Neel didn't retreat to the corner conversation-wise. If the conversation was interesting, she didn't do the nice lady from Pennsylvania thing and stand along the margins of thought while the guys got to have the language and the thoughts. Part of her brilliance was her ability to throw body and soul into the arguments of the day. Her apartment, while being filled with her work, was also filled with language, books by Lenin and Marx along with novels and plays, a galaxy of words hovering near her gallery of faces. She was never without politics, and it was the politics I saw and experienced in life that opened me up further to what Neel was doing in portraits like *Henry Geldzahler*: talking about class. And how Henry's labor was about taste, and how being an arbiter of taste can be distancing and deforming, especially if it's removed from the real world of politics and blood. And it almost always is.

Once, a gay artist told me that when he was a student Neel came to his school to give a talk. When she found out that the students knew little if anything about Chile and Pinochet's reign, and America's involvement, she got very, very angry, saying, "How can you be an artist and not know about politics?" For a long time I thought that being gay was politics enough—difficult enough—but then when I looked at Neel's portraits of Jackie Curtis and others, I saw the disaster and beauty inherent in becoming a self and realized it occurs not only within the subject's body, but in the eye of the world. I loved Geldzahler and others for their outright queerness even as I recoiled from their love of hierarchy and power. Neel's portraits of queer thinkers, artists, and beings taught me that what I was drawing back from, ultimately, was affect, and what I was looking for—what Alice Neel painted—was the collective uncanny: how, despite the odds, we persisted in being a self no matter how you or the world labeled it.

PLATES

Martin Jay, 1932
Oil on canvas
25 × 20 ¼ inches
63.5 × 51.4 cm

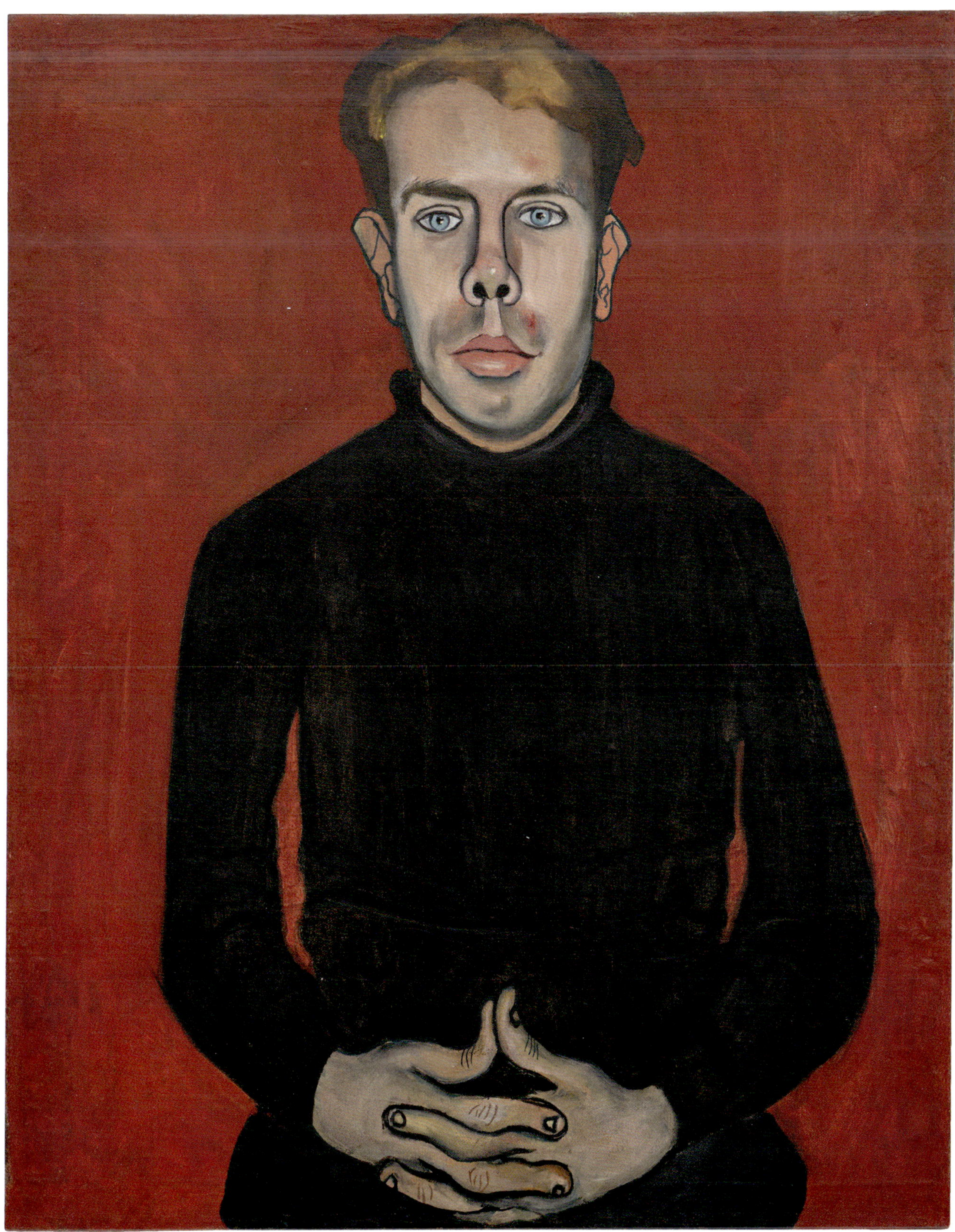

Christopher Lazare, 1932
Watercolor and collage on paper
12 3/8 × 9 1/4 inches
31.4 × 23.5 cm

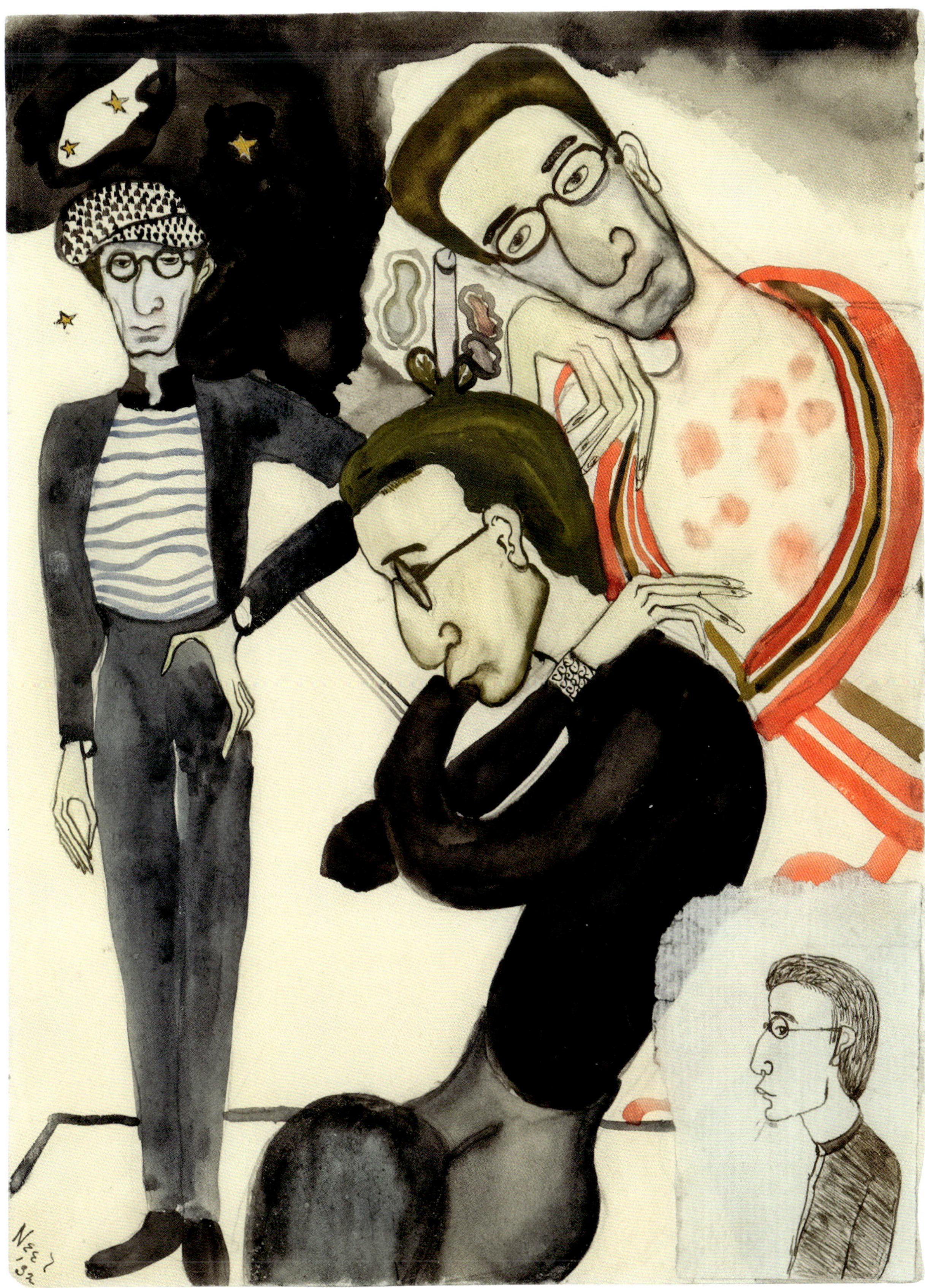
Neel
'32

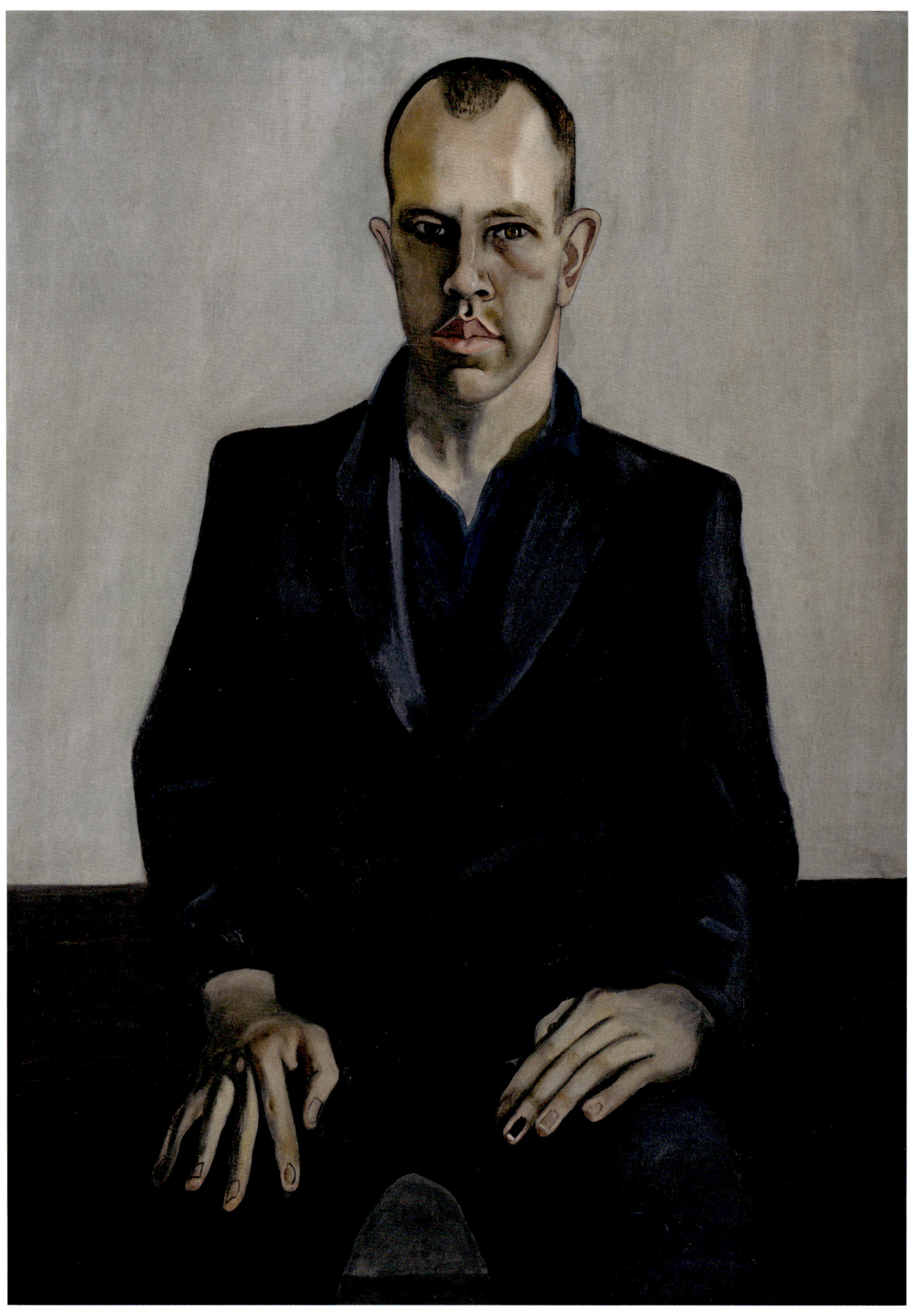

Max White, 1935
Oil on canvas
36 × 26 inches
91.4 × 66 cm

Al Freer, 1946
Oil on canvas
32 × 22 inches
81.3 × 55.9 cm

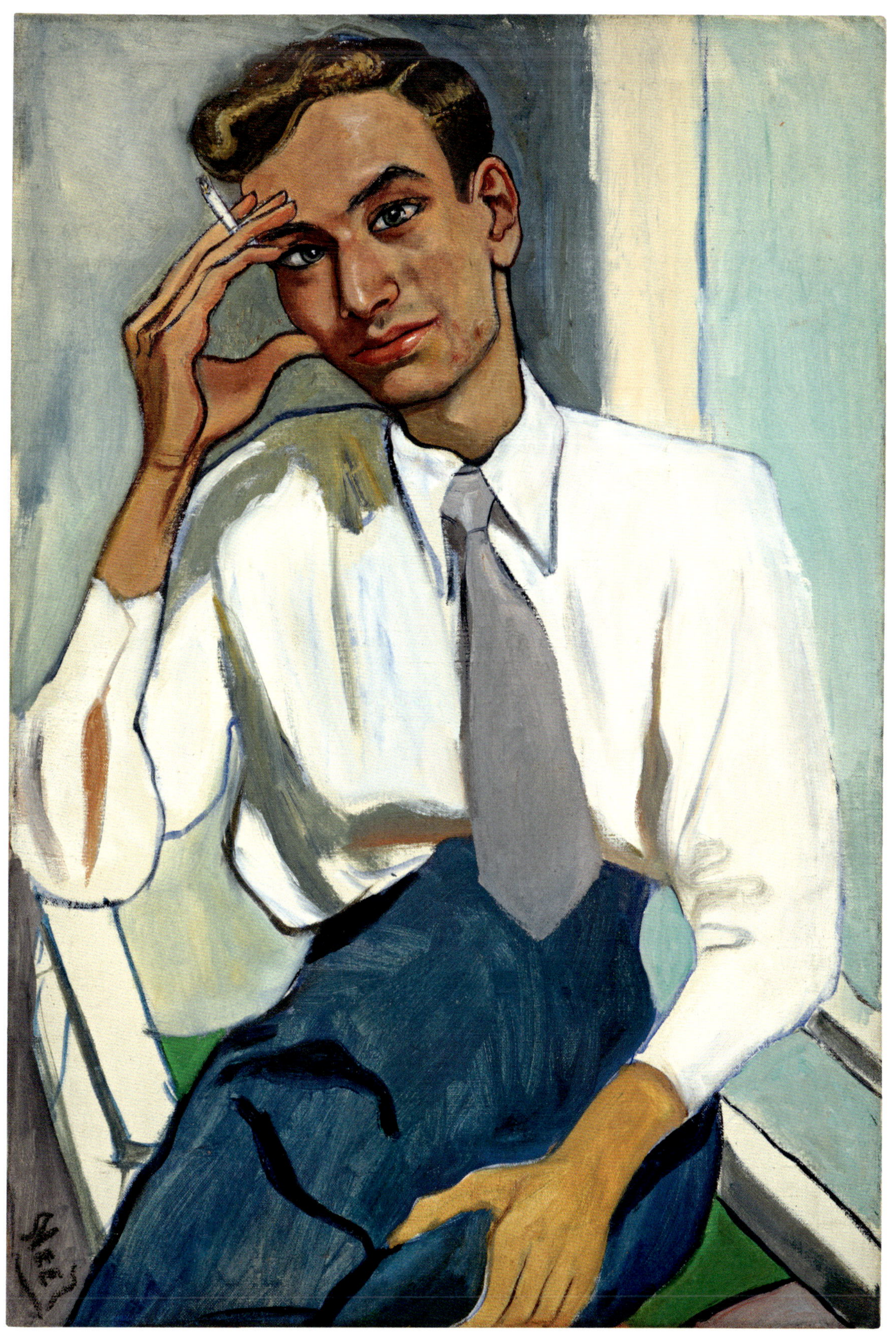

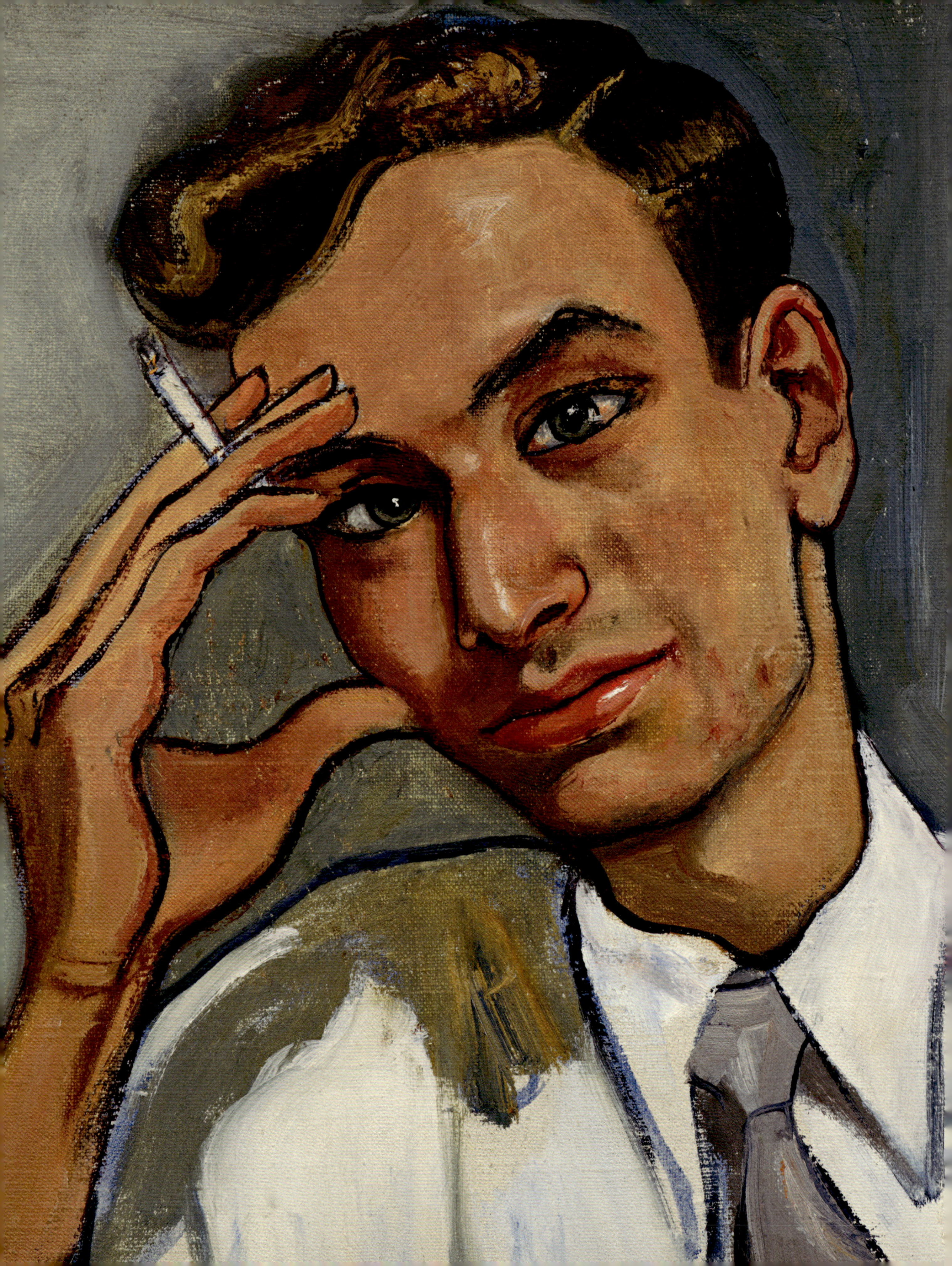

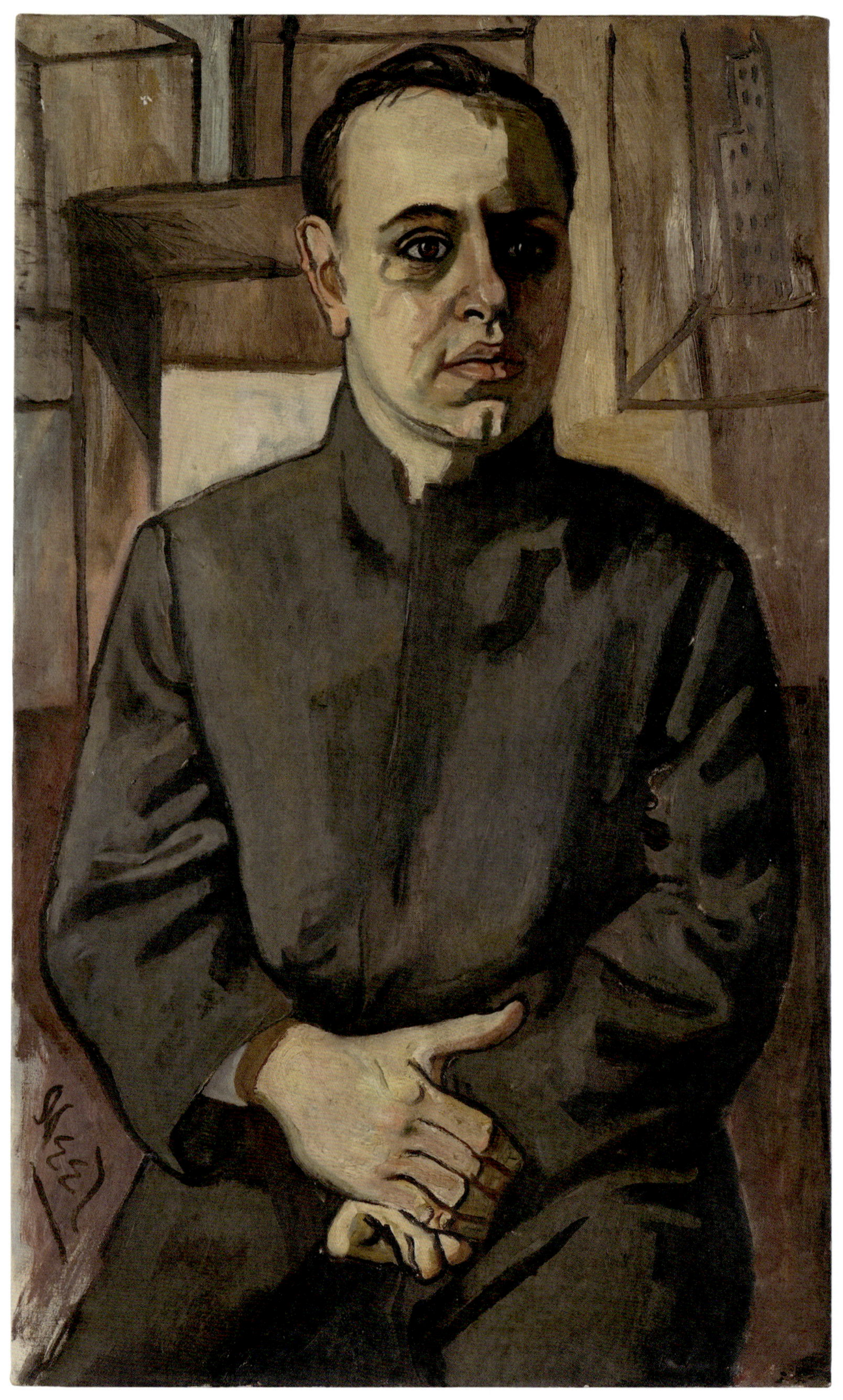

Paul Kuyer, 1959
Oil on canvas
36 × 22 inches
91.4 × 55.9 cm

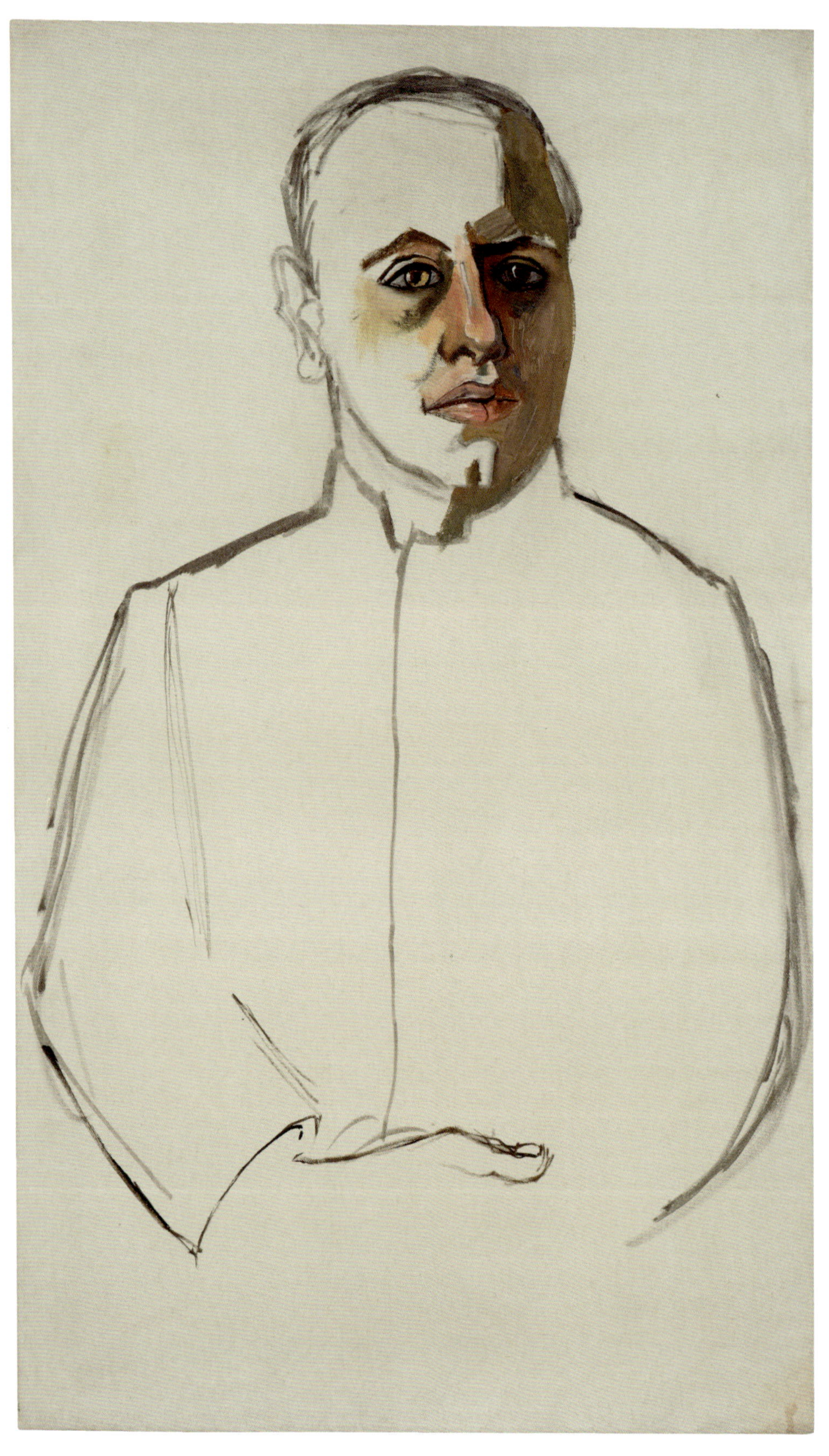

Paul Kuyer, 1959
Oil on canvas
34 × 20 ⅛ inches
86.4 × 51.1 cm

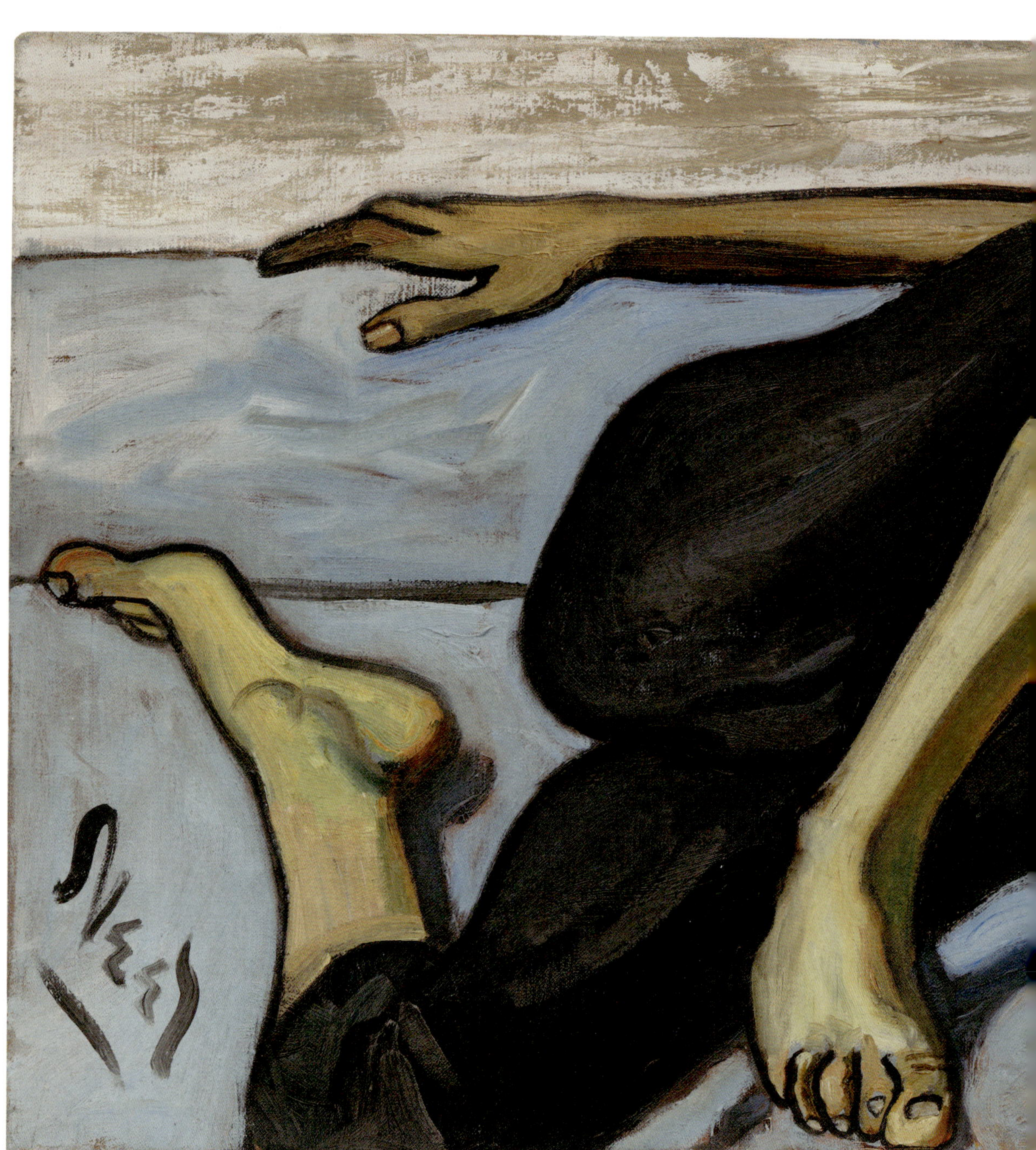

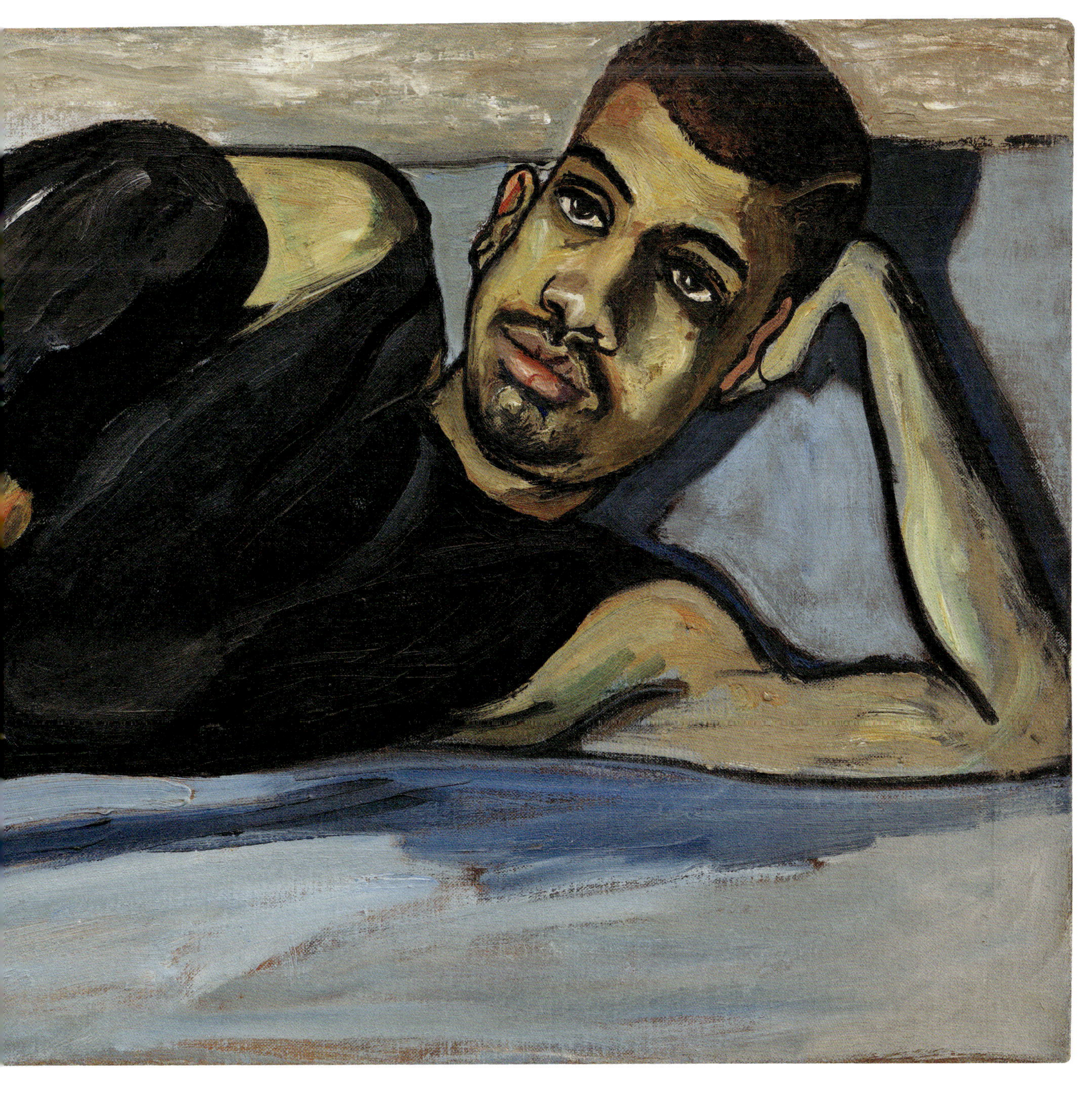

Ballet Dancer, 1950
Oil on canvas
20 1/8 × 42 1/8 inches
51.1 × 107 cm

Frank O'Hara No. 2, 1960
Oil on canvas
38 × 24 inches
96.5 × 61 cm

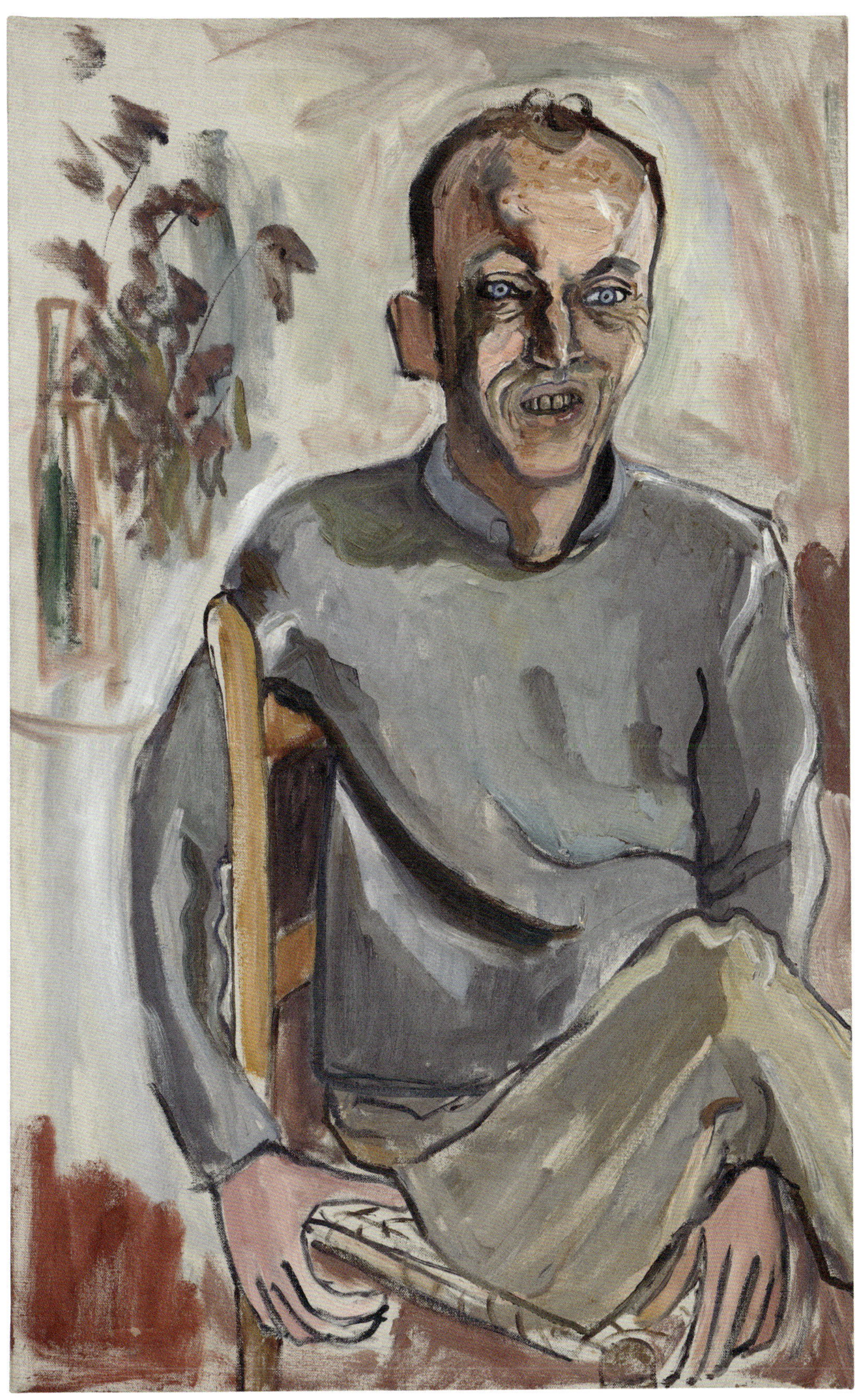

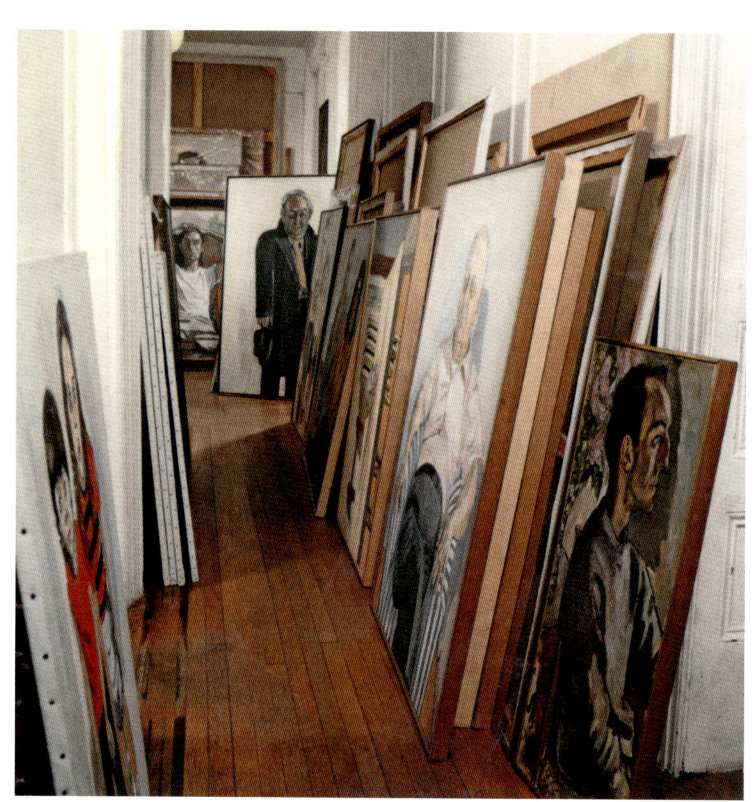

Paintings in Alice Neel's home on West 107th Street, New York, after 1965

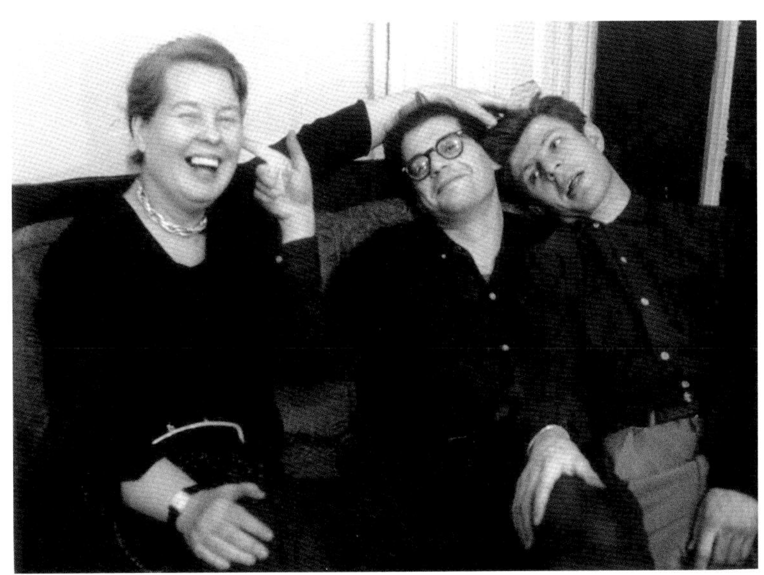

Alice Neel with Allen Ginsberg and Peter Orlovsky on the set of *Pull My Daisy*, 1959

Allen Ginsberg, 1966
Oil on canvas
50 × 35 ¼ inches
127 × 89.5 cm

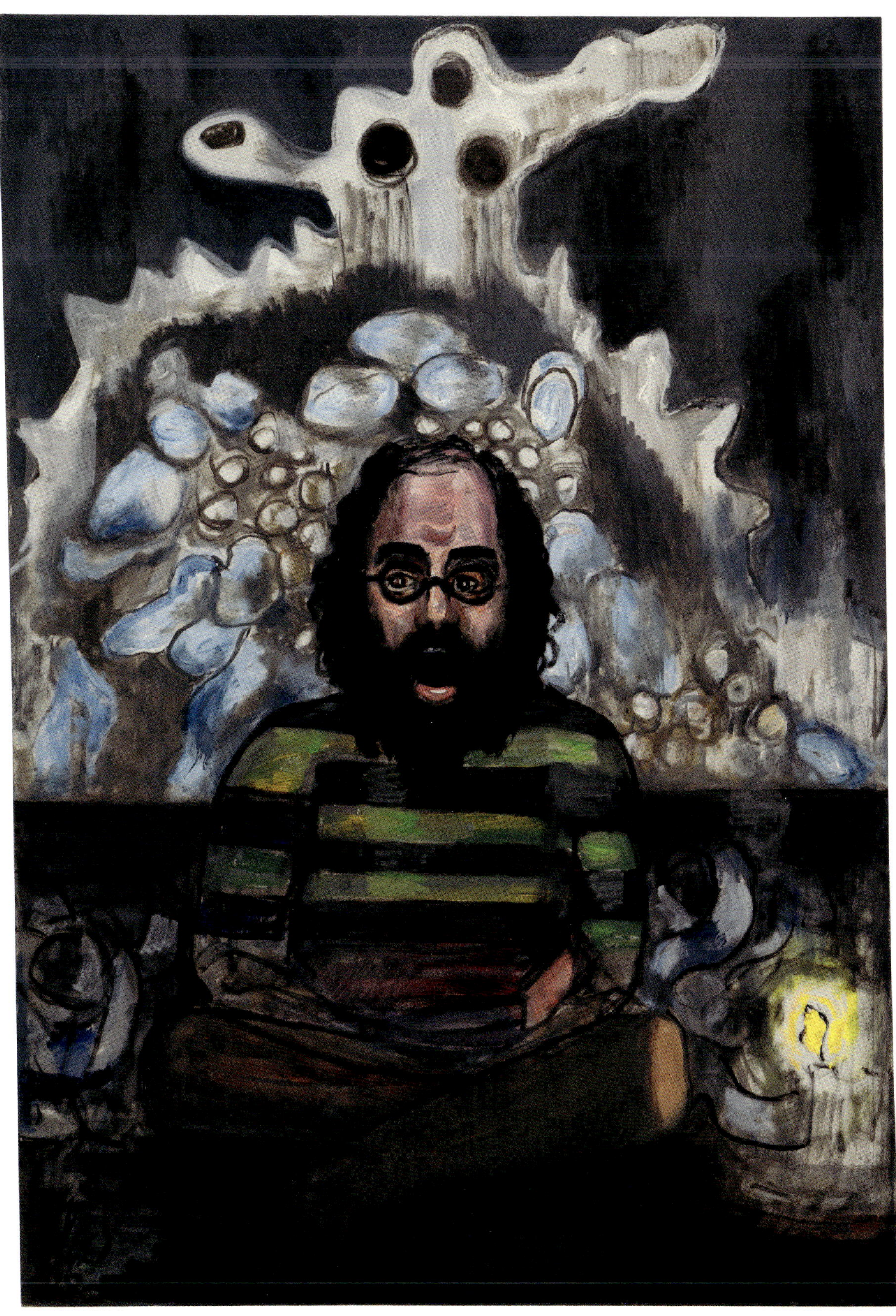

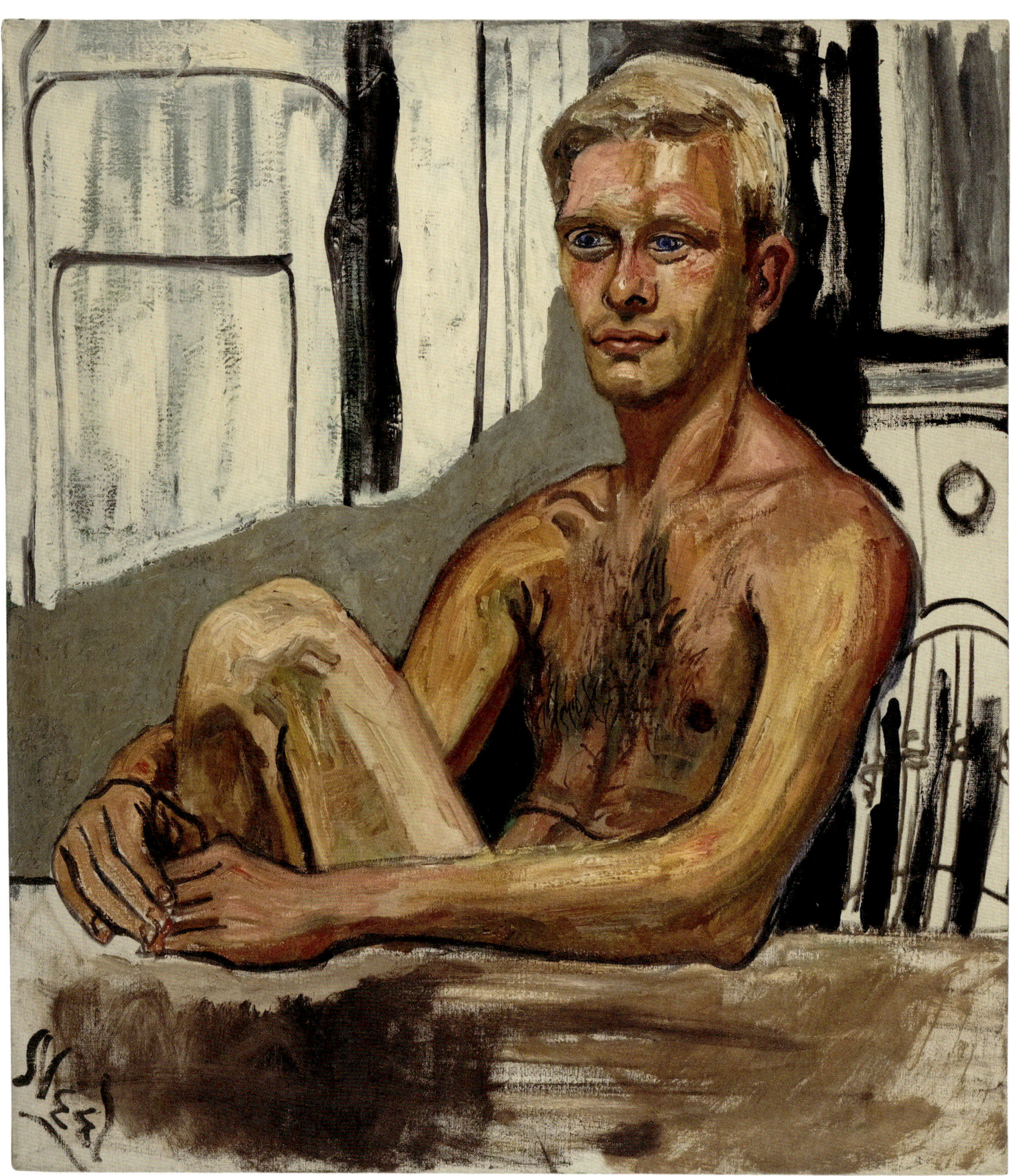

Richard Gibbs, 1965
Oil on canvas
38 × 34 inches
96.5 × 86.4 cm

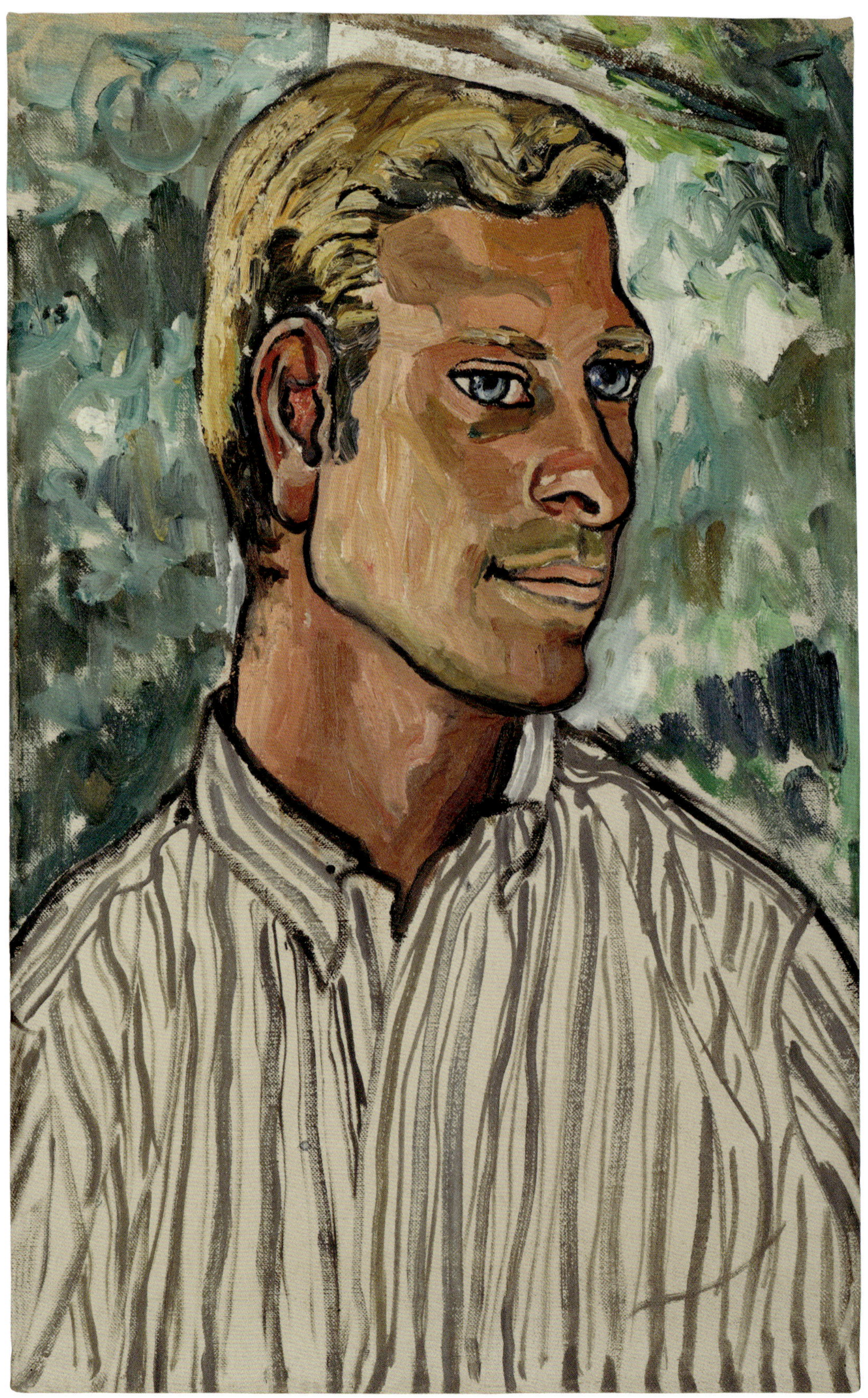

Richard Gibbs, 1961
Oil on canvas
25 × 16 inches
63.5 × 40.6 cm

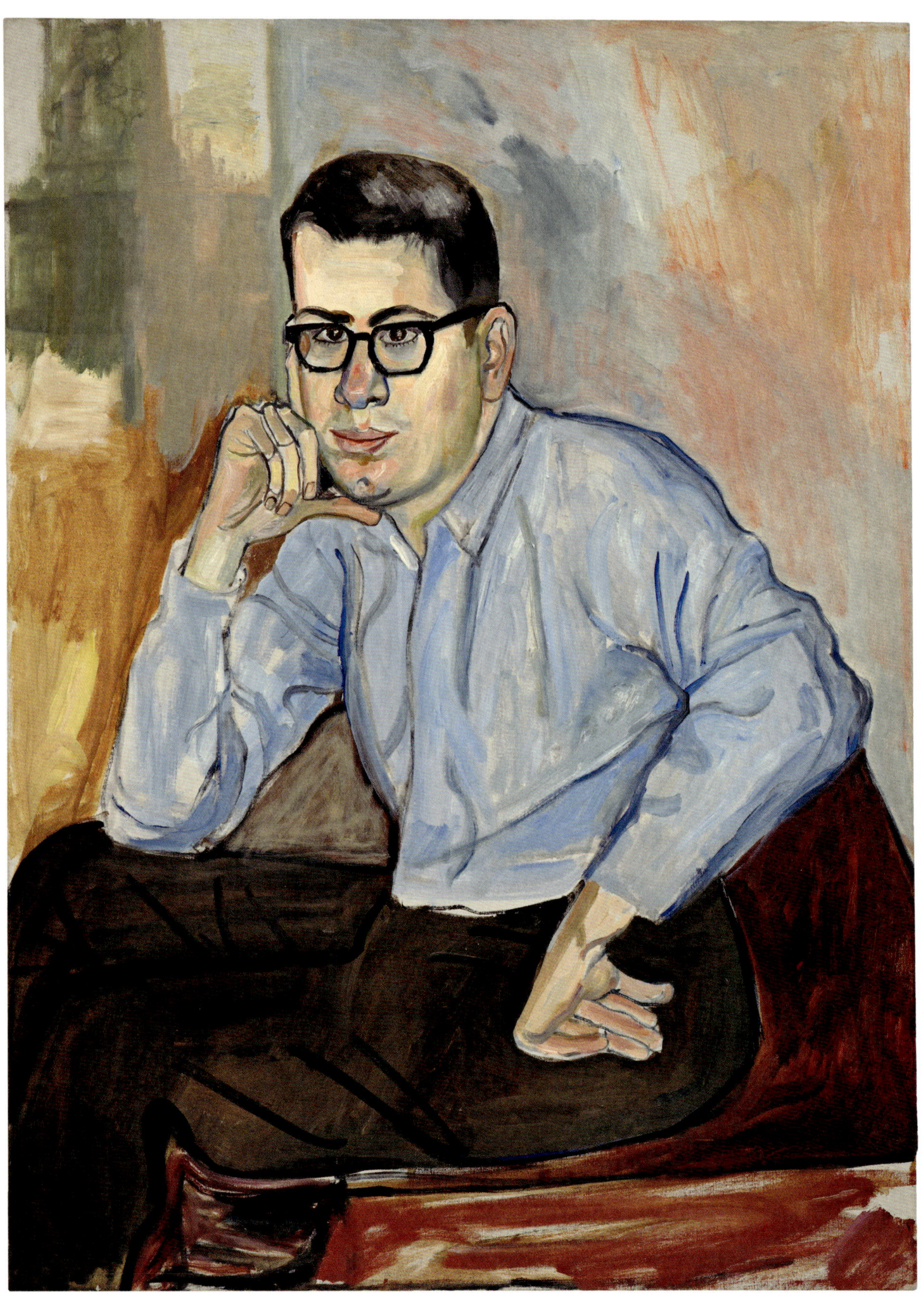

Richard Gibbs' Friend, c. 1962
Oil on canvas
42 × 31 inches
106.7 × 78.7 cm

Arthur Bullowa, c. 1960
Oil on canvas
40 × 27 inches
101.6 × 68.6 cm

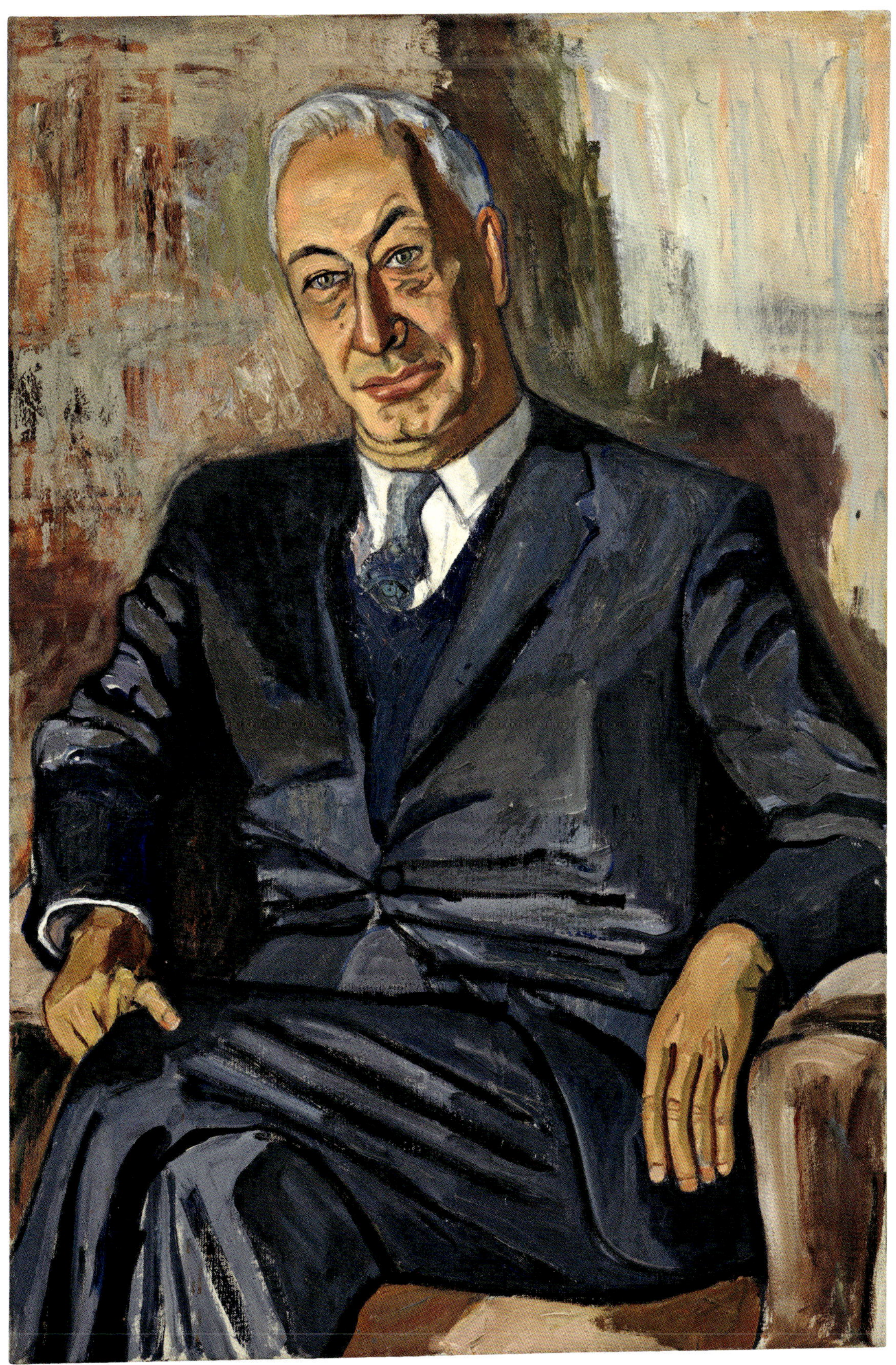

William Walton, 1967
Oil on canvas
48 × 33 inches
121.9 × 83.8 cm

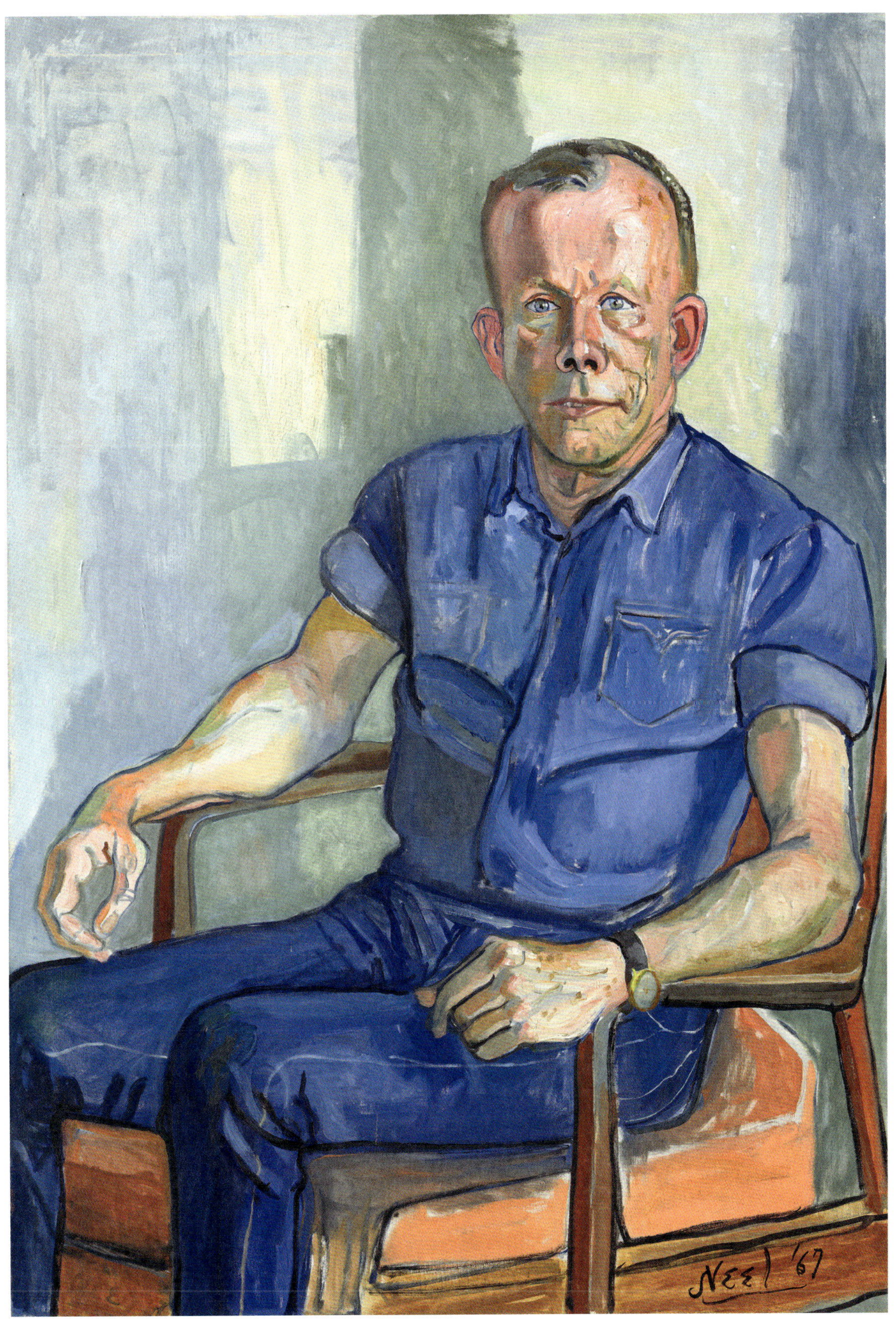
Neel '67

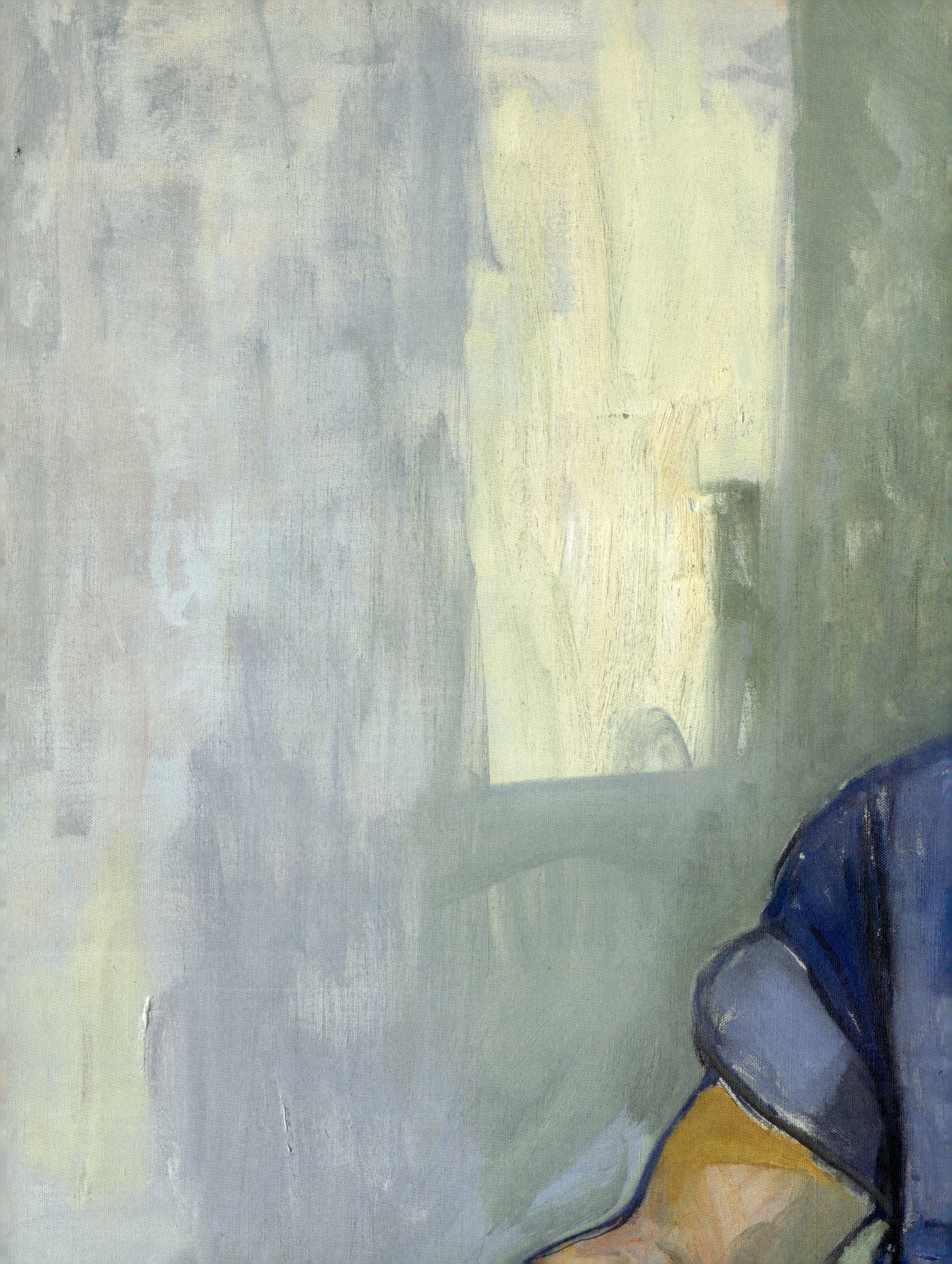

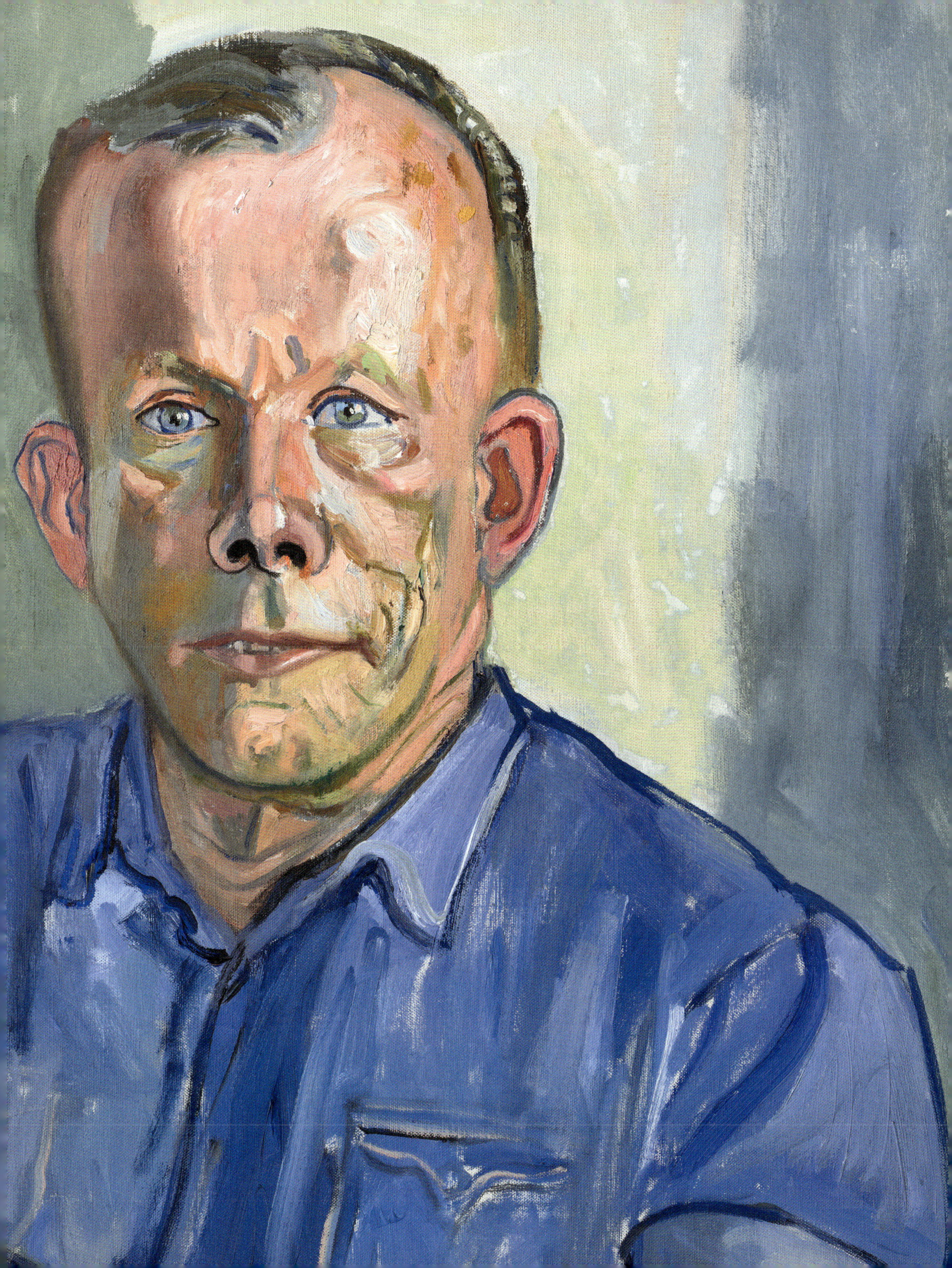

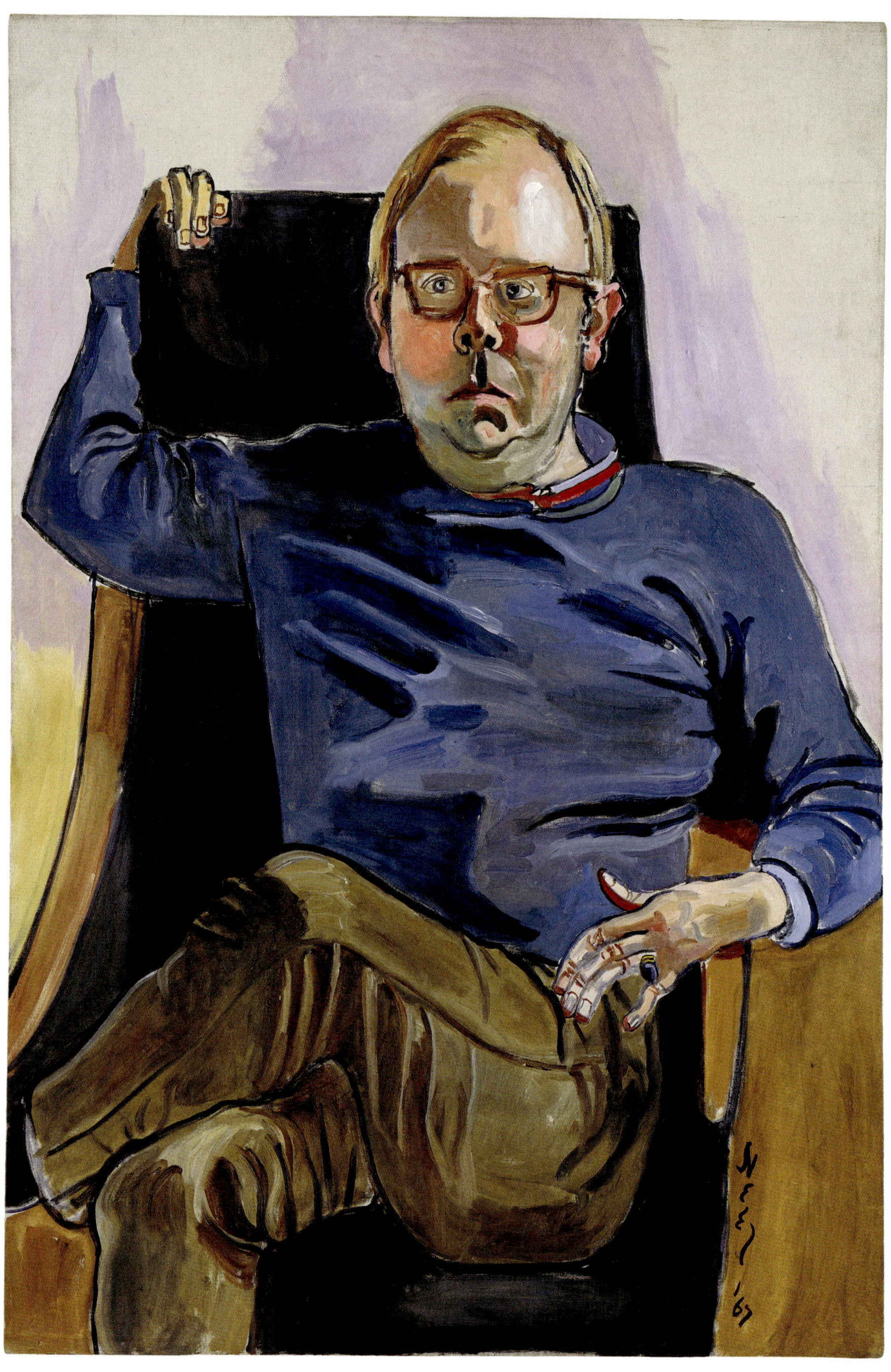
NEEL
'67

Henry Geldzahler, 1967
Oil on canvas
50 × 33 ⅞ inches
127 × 86 cm

Rose Fried's Nephew, 1963
Oil on canvas
38 × 24 inches
96.5 × 61 cm

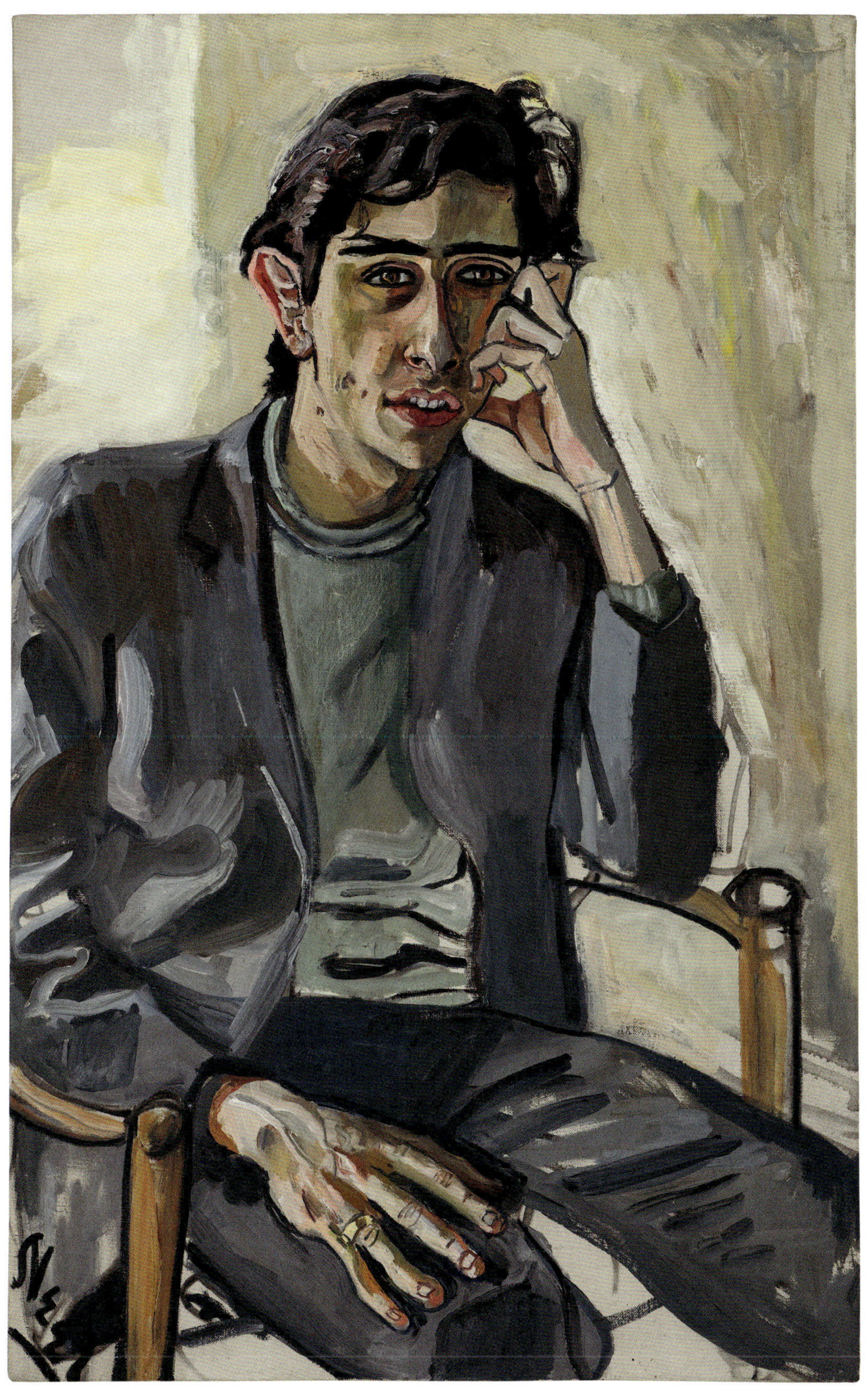

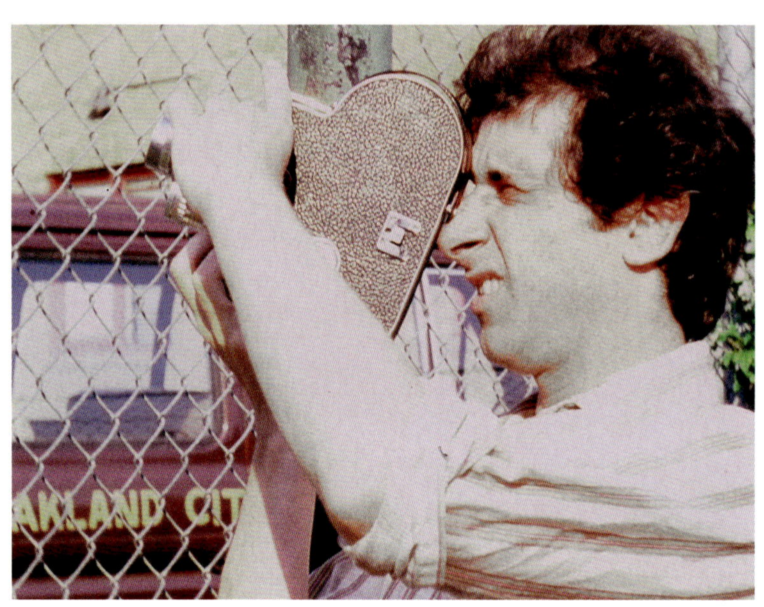

Roger Jacoby, 1978. Still from the film *Elegy in the Streets* by Jim Hubbard, 1989

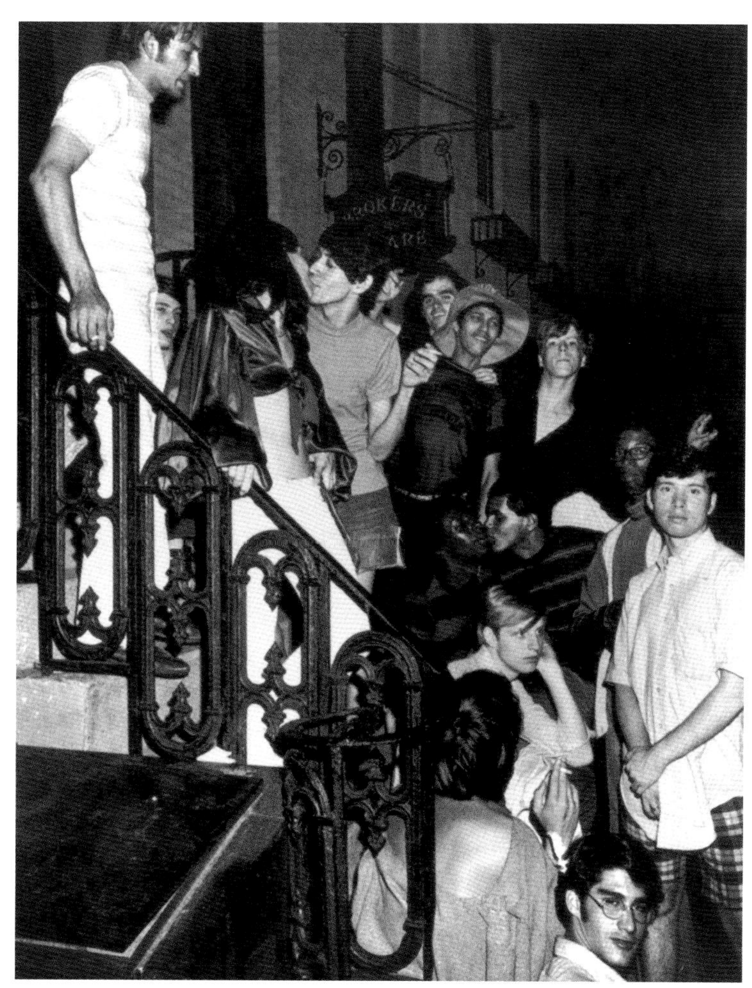

Stonewall celebrations, 1969. Photo by Fred McDarrah

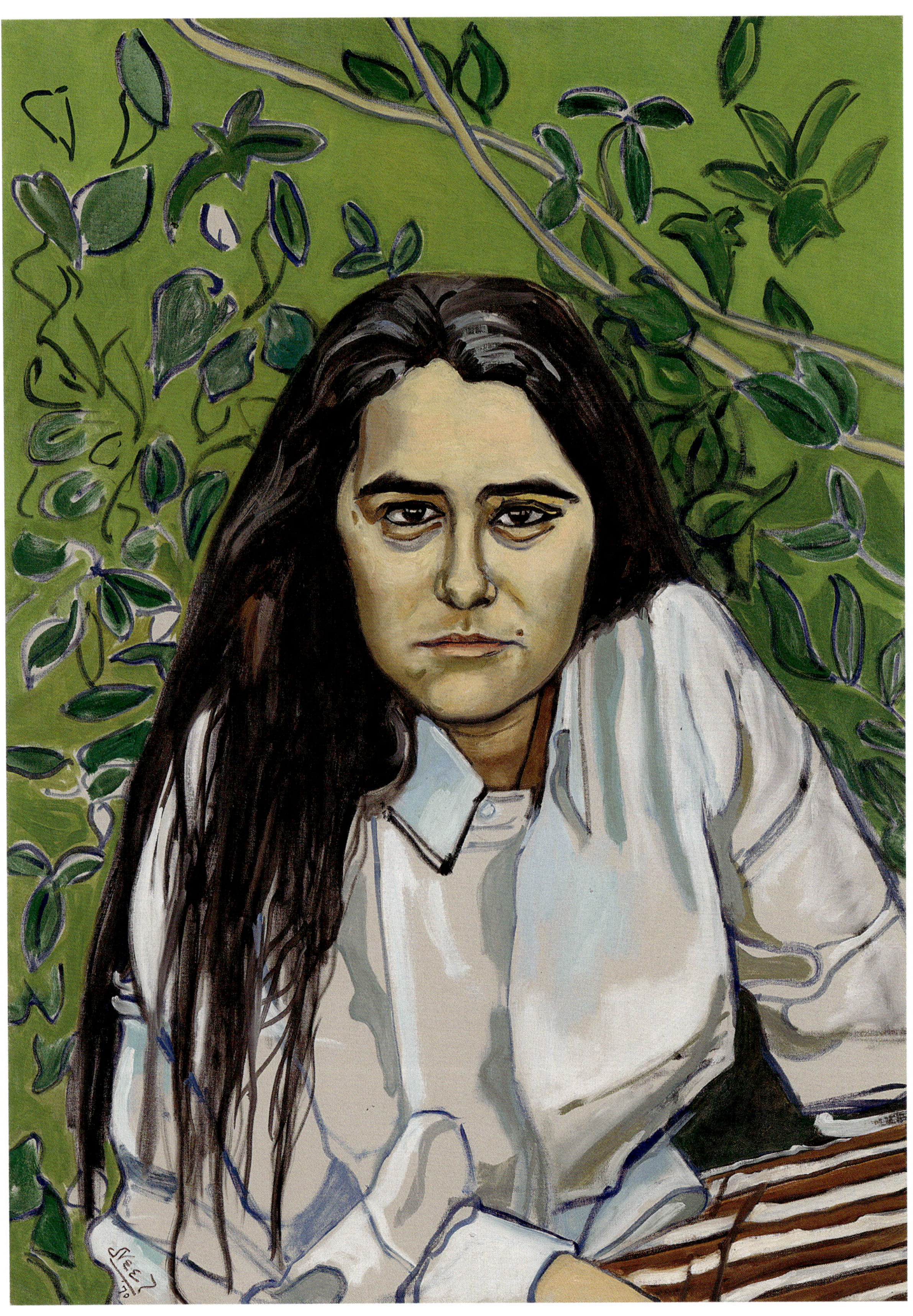

Kate Millett, 1970
Oil on canvas
39 ¾ × 28 ½ inches
101 × 72.4 cm

Andy Warhol, c. 1970
Ink, graphite, and gouache on
tracing paper mounted on paper
6 ⅛ × 4 ¼ inches
15.6 × 10.8 cm

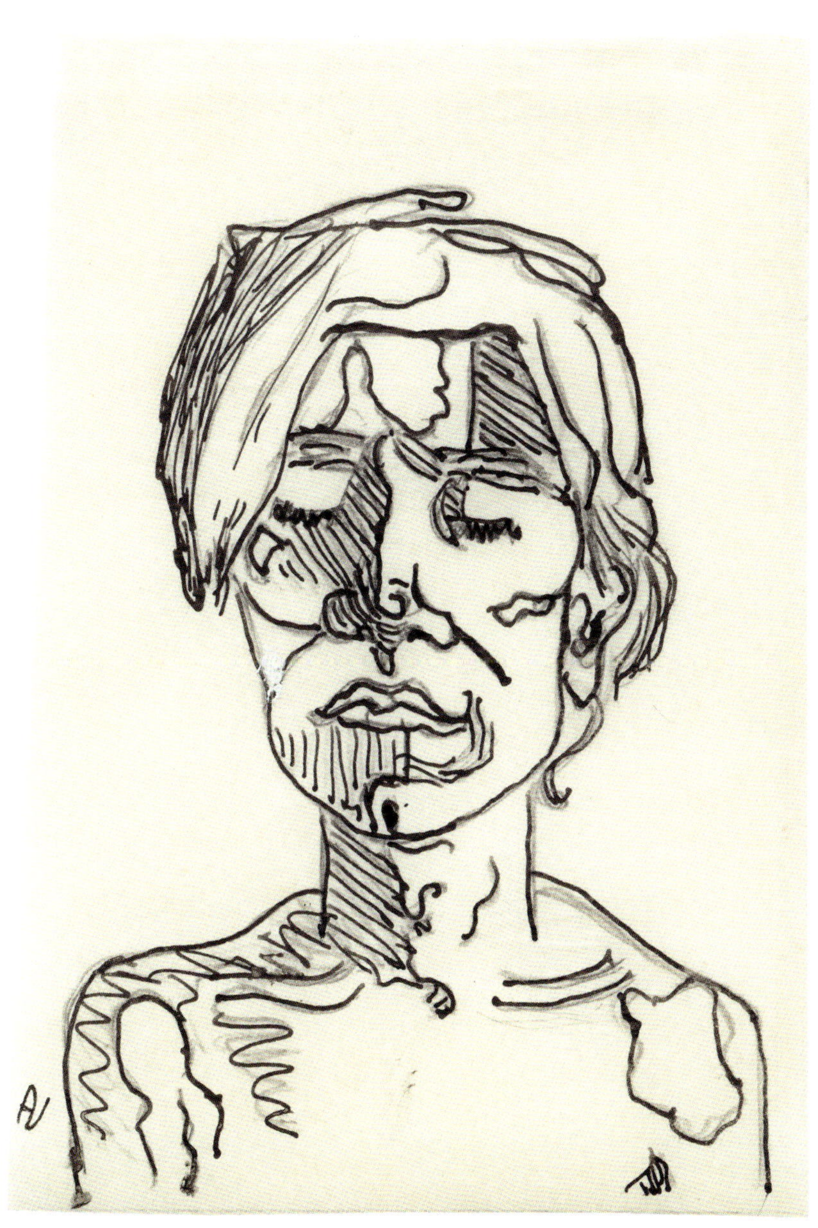

Jackie Curtis and Ritta Redd, 1970
Oil on canvas
60 × 41 7/8 inches
152.4 × 106.4 cm

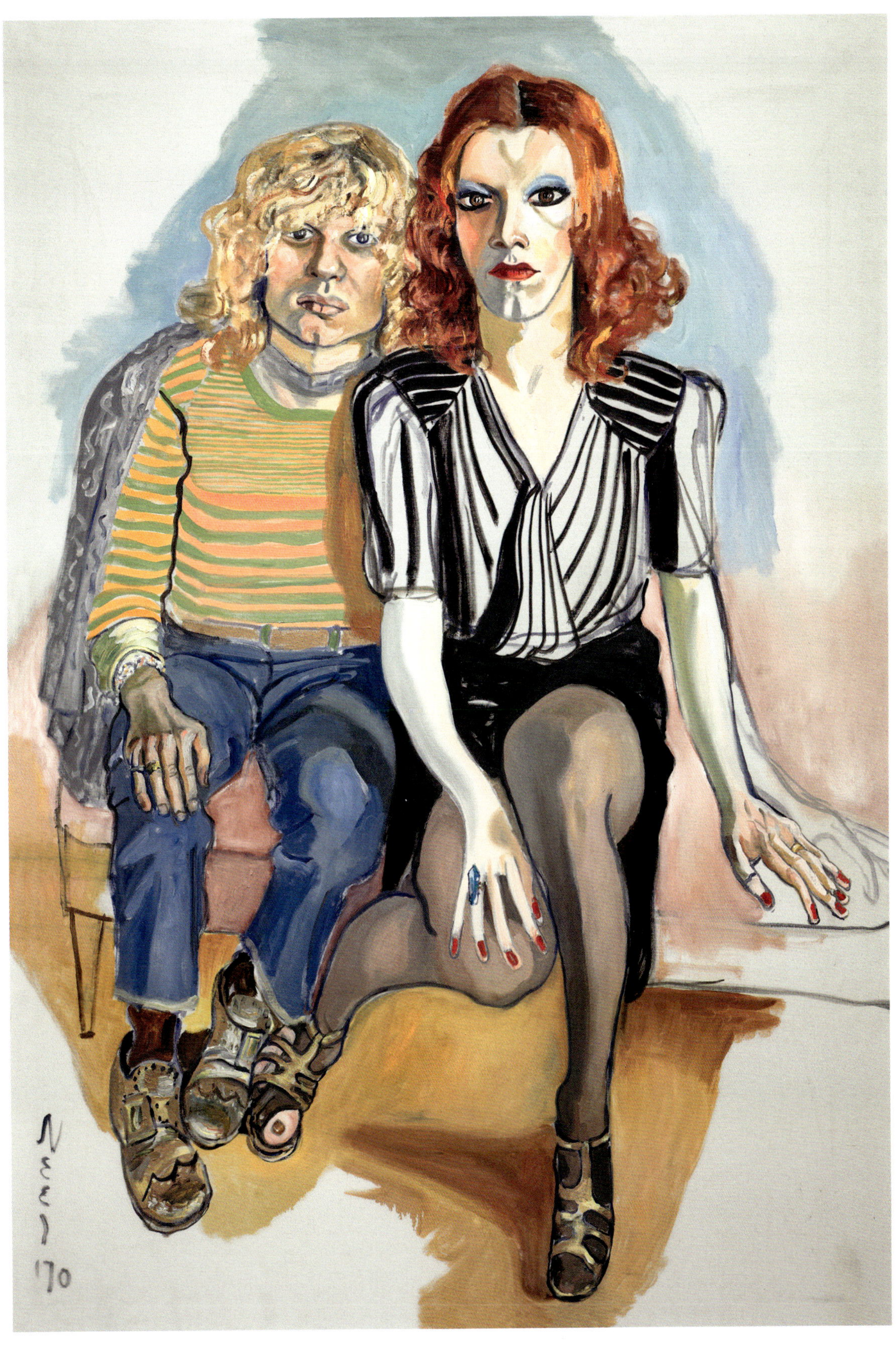
NEEL
'70

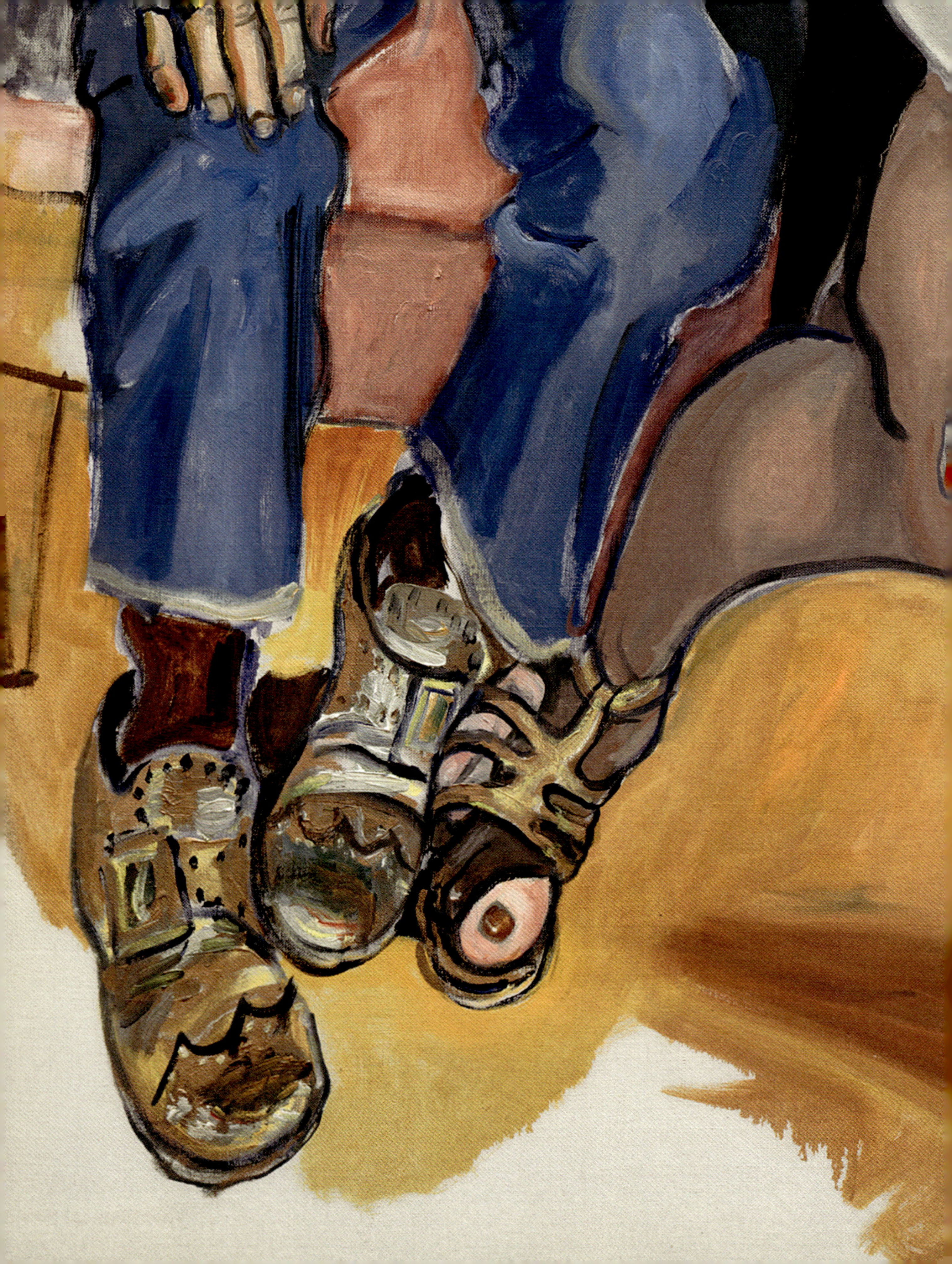

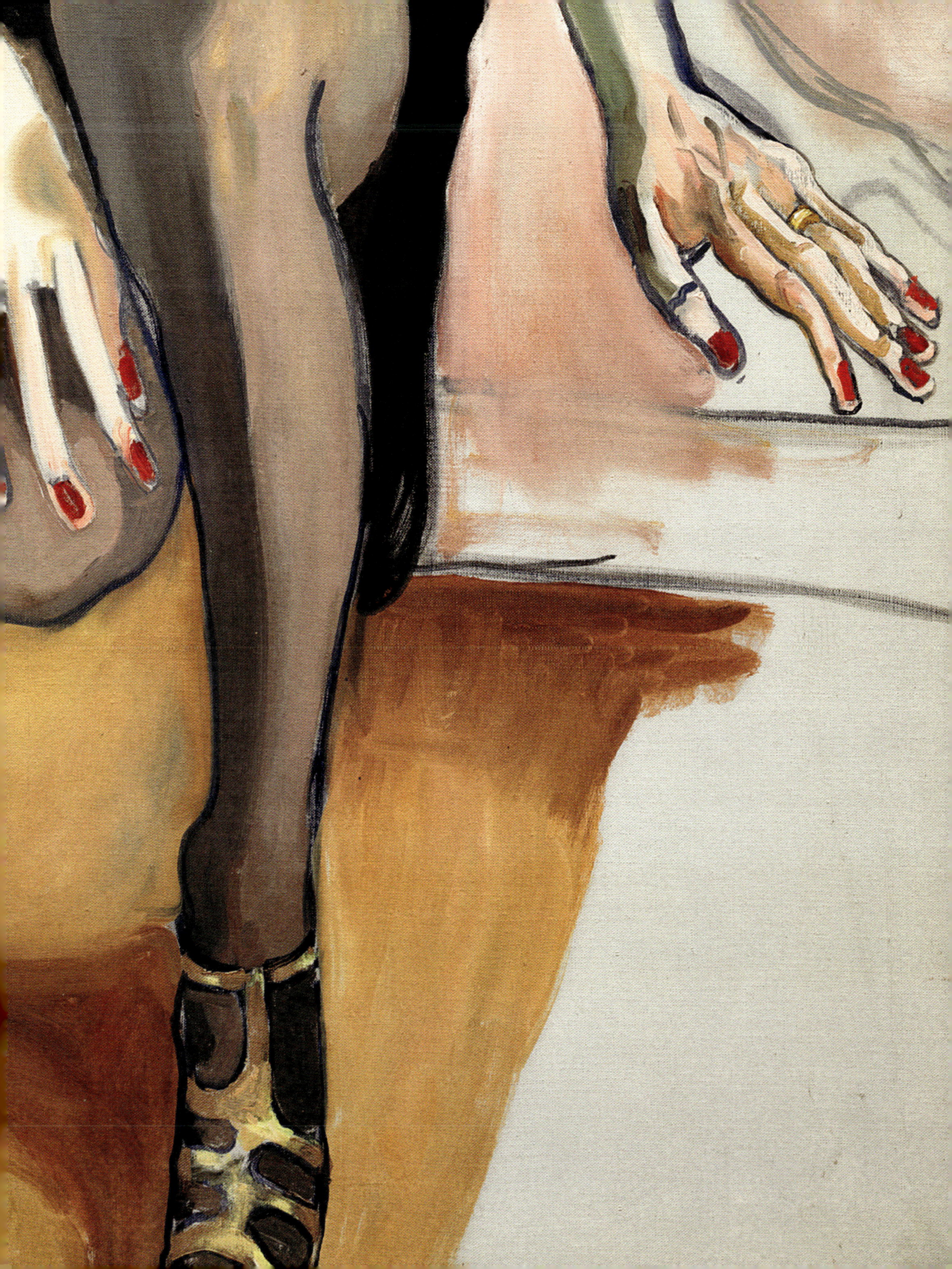

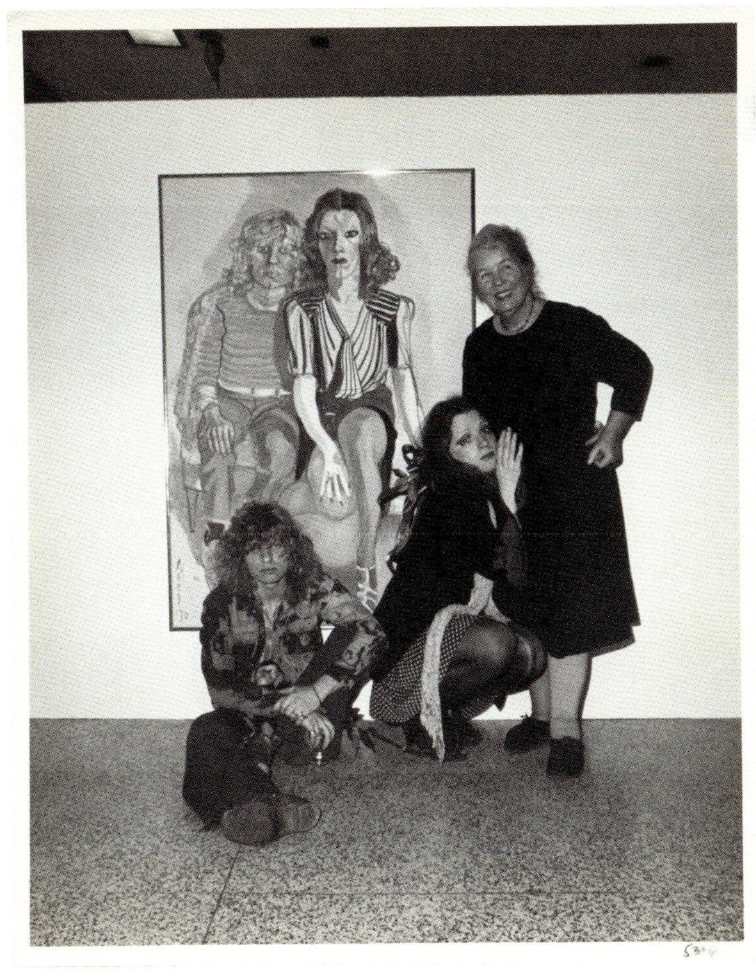

Ritta Redd, Jackie Curtis, and Alice Neel at *Alice Neel: A Comprehensive Exhibition of Paintings, 1930–1970*, Moore College of Art, Philadelphia, 1971

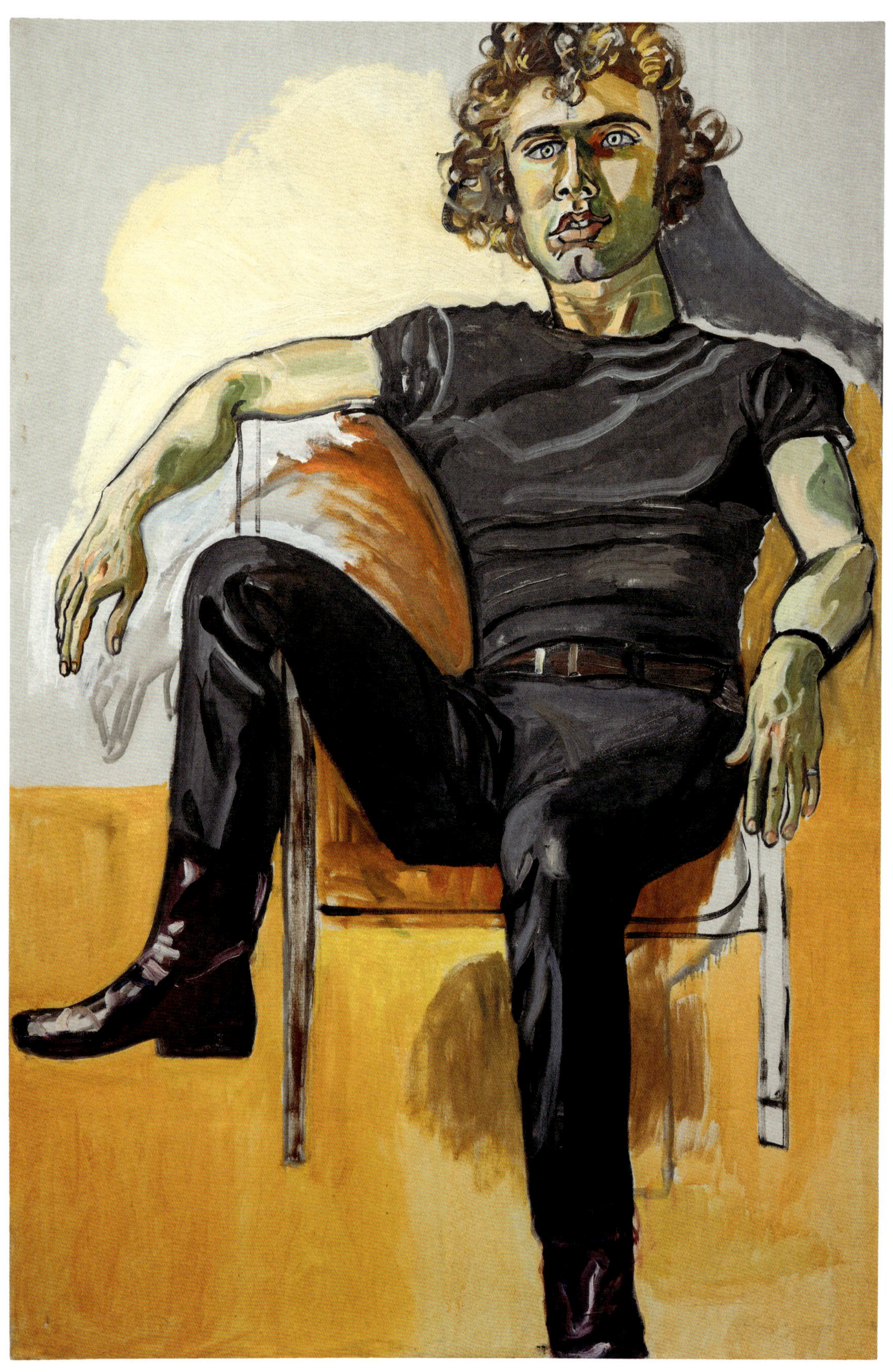

Gerard Malanga, 1969
Oil on canvas
60 × 40 inches
152.4 × 101.6 cm

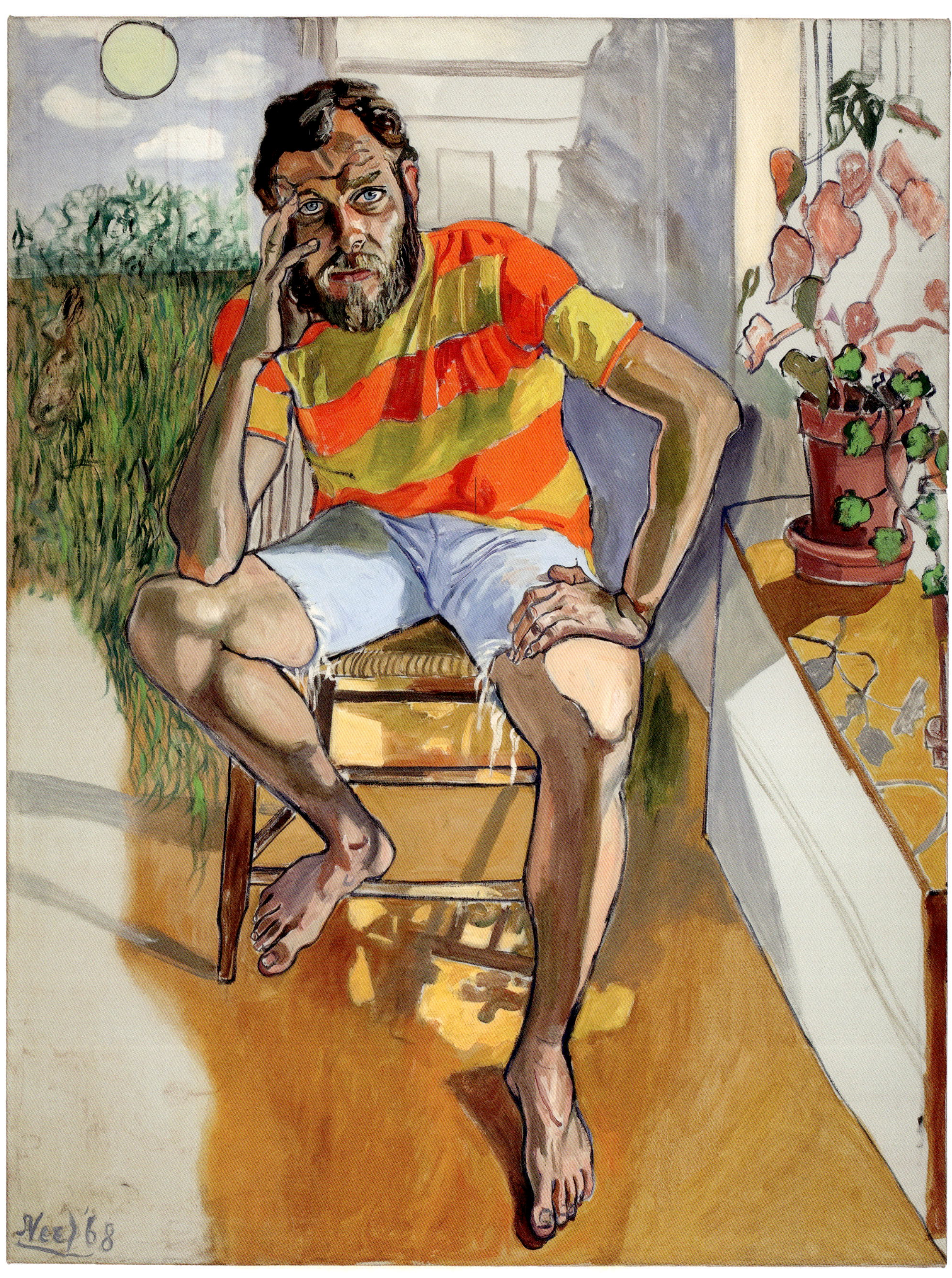

Richard Gibbs, 1968
Oil on canvas
64 × 50 inches
162.6 × 127 cm

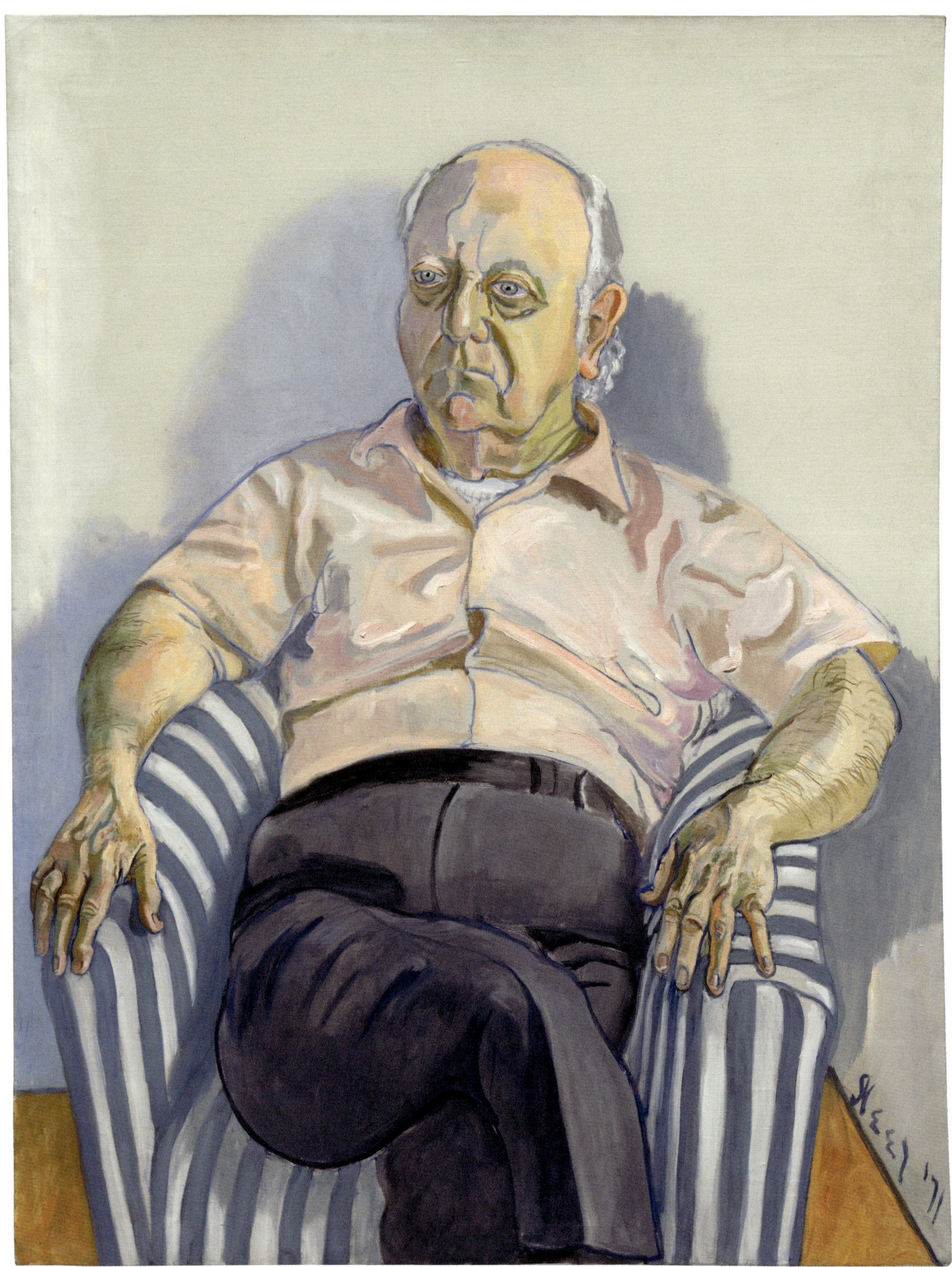

Virgil Thomson, 1971
Oil on canvas
47 ½ × 36 ½ inches
120.7 × 92.7 cm

Robert Avedis Hagopian, 1971
Oil on canvas
46 × 29 ¾ inches
116.8 × 75.6 cm

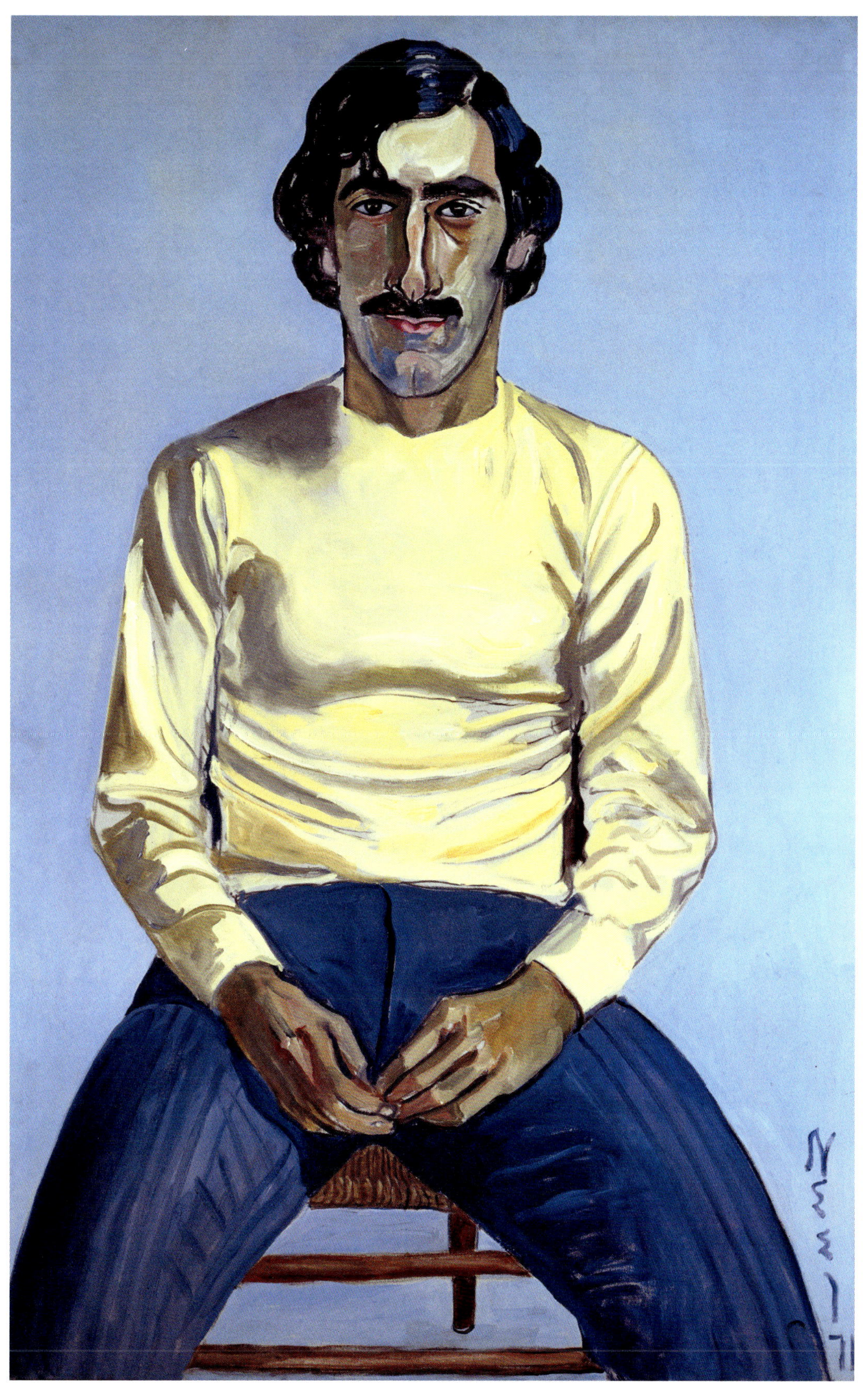

WAYNE KOESTENBAUM

LECTURE ON NOTHING; OR, GAYS SHOULD BE NICE TO EACH OTHER

my gay friend and I mirthfully agree that gays are not nice to each other

this lecture's verboten thesis statement is that gays are not nice to each other but that Alice Neel, in her paintings, was nice to gays

"nice" is a gay word because it is devalued, flattened, glossily all-purpose

the vowel in "nice" is open to being stretched and played with

I don't know what "gay" means, and not everyone that Alice Neel painted was gay

I could find other, better, more recent words, but the phenomenon of gay-to-gay unkindness requires the outdated word "gay"

no need to bring up examples of gays not being nice to each other

such incidents are legion

I wish I could focus on Alice Neel's portrait of Geoffrey Hendricks and Brian Buczak but I am predisposed instead to taking detours

in the portrait of Geoffrey and Brian, why only now do I see bananas?

notice when suddenly the depicted body offers an eroticism that makes us nervous

Neel consecrates our couture, our codes, and the complicit, inadmissible gleam in our eyes

have you ever anointed a certain painting as *yours* because you desire its subject and want to make a specific claim upon it?

a gay look might presuppose a dram of beauty (forced or given) and

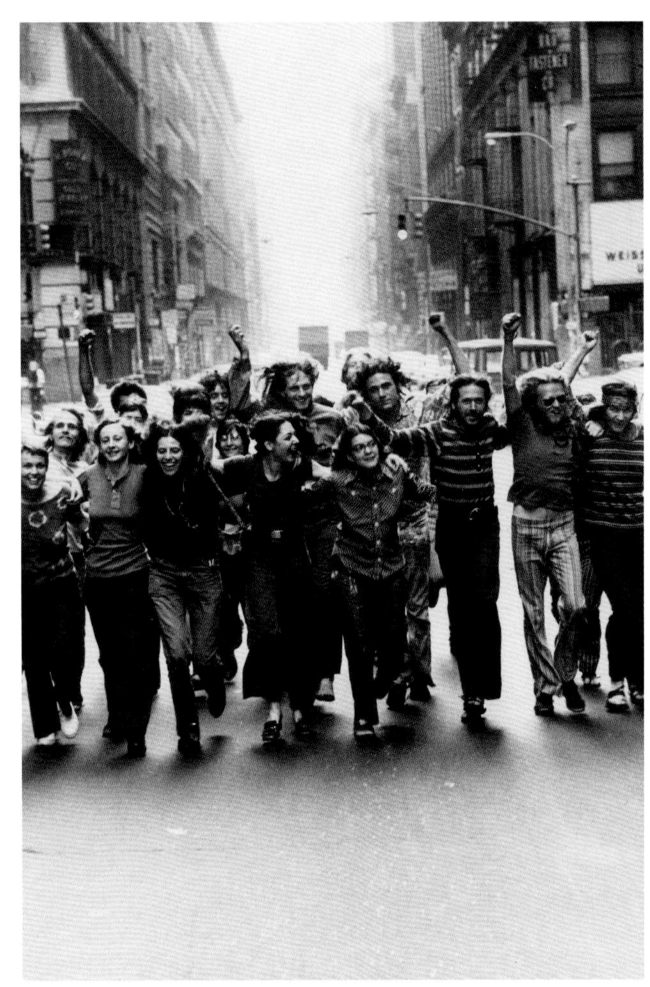

Peter Hujar, *Gay Liberation Front Poster Image*, 1969

extra vigilance over outfit choice but also the imposition of a wall—a froideur—to protect against rebuke

I imagine that these men wouldn't have liked me

the sitters flee or retreat into their chairs

sometimes a chair intensifies the sitter's cuteness

hands encapsulate the allure but also siphon it off, struggle against it

Neel, a sympathetic spelunker, is being auto-investigated by her own portraying hand

the painting's elements, like the materials of a short story, must exist at oblique angles to each other, without clumsy exposition

in Neel's portrait of John Cheim, incompletion intensifies his ocular plea

seeing the 1979 portrait of a figure named Cuchulain, I murmur, "oh, that one is deep"

what do I mean by "deep"?

"deep" defers delving

when we call lips "prissy," are we revering or rejecting them?

before they entreat, prissy lips accuse

in Neel's portrait of Robbie Tillotson giving the peace sign, she captured a sexual dissidence at ease with its own directness and thus capable of finding, in candor, a rest cure

in the portrait of David and Catherine Saalfield, David's louche look summons the unfixed camaraderie of Liza Minnelli and Wendell Burton in *The Sterile Cuckoo*

Neel's paintings set up a hunger to know (a hunger to Google?) lost hotness

she aimed to capture smoldering but not caption it

must I commit the vulgarity of classifying it?

she stuns and exalts the figures by outlining them in ultramarine

outlining is frowned upon, though Picasso and Matisse, among others, loved to draw borders around shapes, as if to protect them against mental confusion

when Neel outlines, she traps the figure, which can glow with redoubled intensity because caged

the figure will stare at you motionlessly for a time you could call unendurable ("An unendurable age," wrote John Ashbery in an early poem)

a few decades ago a megalomaniacal aesthete stared across a café table at me so protractedly that I relinquished volition

Neel's instinct for defamiliarization and detachment allowed her to limn the nonhuman, if a blue striped armchair qualifies as nonhuman

she often tilts forward the perspective, "serving up" the figures to us—like labile Catherine Holly (Liz Taylor) procuring tricks for her gay cousin Sebastian Venable in *Suddenly, Last Summer*

"Marxist Girl" (Irene Peslikis) sits on an anti-realistic chair that slides me into déjà vu, as if a viewer's psychological state retroactively underwrote a painting's divergence from verisimilitude

in Neel's 1932 watercolor of Christopher Lazare, she renders him as rebukingly thin, with elongated hands, a bracelet, splotches on his chest, and a nose so big it's a caricature (exaggeration may signal respect)

Martin Jay, 1932, who are you, austere, frontal, theatrical, in black turtleneck, shaving cut or rouged blemish above your lip?

in Neel's rendering of Dennis Florio, with handlebar moustache and red velvet suit, he looks like Proust, eyes burning their *durée* into us

in a *New York* magazine article, Annie Sprinkle called Florio the "picture framer to the stars"

do I assert an attachment to Florio or to Neel—and must I choose?

to whom do I direct my questions, Dennis or Alice?

and do my questions take place in 1978, the date she signs on the painting

or do my questions sing 2023?

does Neel encourage reticence or my usual fatal tendency to spill over logic's limits?

how can a 1978 portrait of a queer person make me jealous?

no language tethers the floating chair

will I exile the longing so that I feel only a detached, analytic relation to the painting's themes?

Robert Avedis Hagopian, classical pianist, you died in 1984

Neel painted you in 1971

you lived in Los Altos then, and I lived nearby

you headed the piano department at University of Santa Clara from 1974 to 1978, and I took a writing course there in 1975

during your reign, I could have tried to take piano lessons from you

your tutelage a forfeited possibility, you occupy (in a feat of daft retrospect) the dead center of my chthonic search for erotic idols

Hagopian, who died of AIDS at age thirty-nine, could be the donnée I build a pederastic narrative around, a fable of a sexy piano teacher and his impressionable, closeted, seventeen-year-old pupil

if I had seen Hagopian in the university lavatory, I would have desired him, and placed him in my Misha Dichter dossier, an oneiric image book (like Pierre Guyotat's "beat sheet") of swarthy pianists

Hagopian, a conglomeration of face, crotch, and hands, teeters off his stool and approaches us

note the folds of Hagopian's long-sleeved cream sweater, at once loose and tight

we treasure the painting's embeddedness in historical time, and we cruise the underworld to find the young man she depicted in 1971

Geoffrey Hendricks and Brian Buczak, I'll return to you now

Buczak, an artist, died of AIDS

the 2018 *New York Times* obituary of Hendricks, a Fluxus artist, mentions Buczak

Hendricks attended John Cage's "Lecture on Nothing" performance in 1950

"Lecture on Nothing"—its commitment to moving beyond literal reference and aesthetic dogma—hovers near Neel's portrait of Hendricks and Buczak

Neel, too, was committed to the nothing

even within figure painting she found a place for the not-specific, for absences that might nourish a mind that longed to veer away from the referent's punishing rivets

Geoff and Brian occasion the portrait, but a painting's secret subject is the nothing it surrounds and reinvents

"gay" itself is a zone of the nothing

and within the ether—funereal nimbus?—of "gay," that mausoleum of a word, can niceness inhere, can niceness find audience or interlocutor?

ignoring someone on a sex app isn't the same as not being nice

ignoring someone at a gay bar isn't the same as not being nice

not establishing eye contact on the street isn't the same as not being nice turning away from someone at a crowded party isn't the same as not being nice

saying catty things online isn't the same as not being nice

refusal of reciprocation isn't the same as not being nice

was Judy Garland nice to Liza?

was Nicholas Ray nice to his wife Gloria Grahame?

Gloria Grahame married Nicholas's son (her former stepson)

sometimes, by ignoring a person, you protect them from your corrosive indifference (hot coffee thrown on Grahame's face in Fritz Lang's *The Big Heat*)

was Pierre Boulez nice to John Cage?

the answer is no

stuff you need to know:

when Neel painted Brian Buczak and Geoffrey Hendricks, Brian was twenty-four and Geoffrey was forty-seven—a noteworthy age difference

Brian, possessor of underground (against-the-grain) masculinity, with shirt unbuttoned and hairy chest, upstages sweater-burdened Geoffrey

when Neel painted their portrait, I was twenty

would Brian have been nice to me, and would I have been nice to Brian?

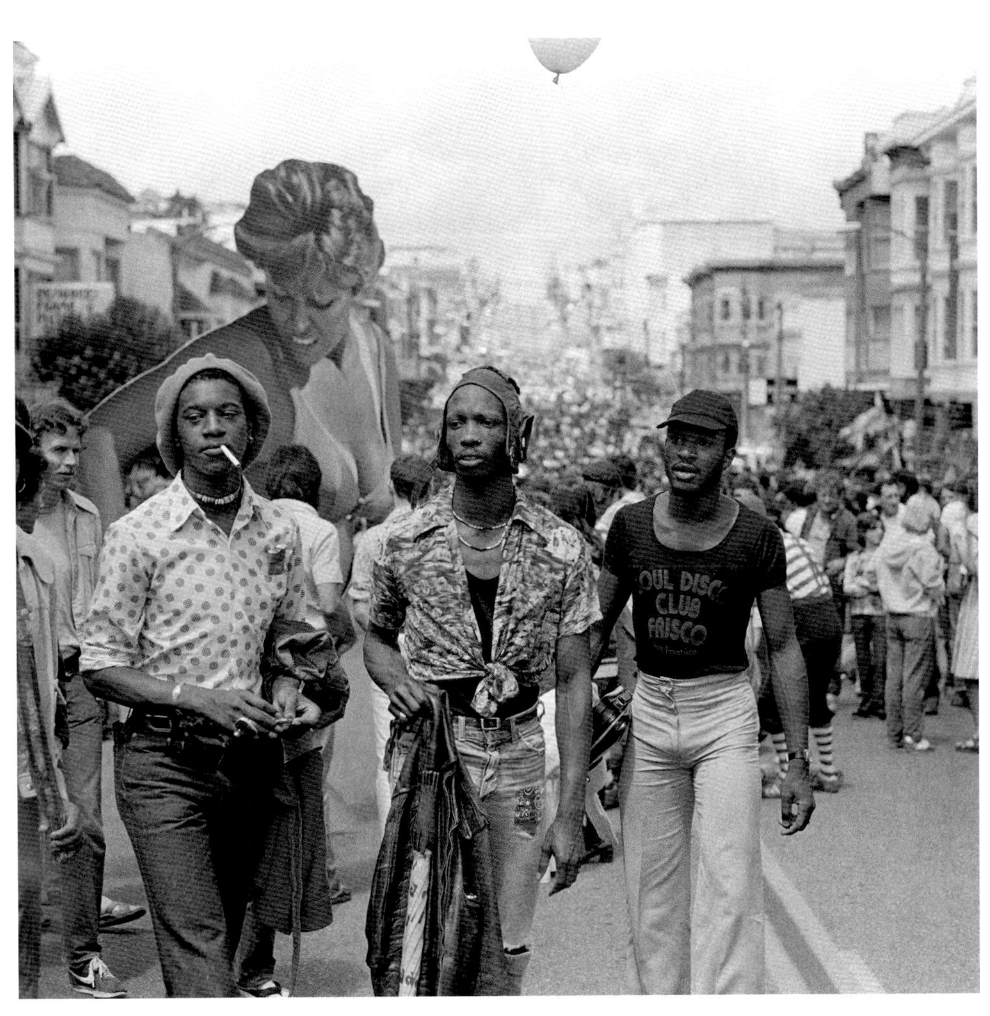

Leon Lott, December Wright, and Larry Williams at the Castro Street Fair, 1976.
Photo by Daniel Nicoletta

when we see this painting, we don't think "Brian is scandalously younger than Geoffrey"

uncontroversially they sport differing modes of coif and confidence

spin the lazy Susan and reach for another dream condiment

I find a reference to Dennis Florio (the man who looks like Proust) in *The New York Times*, April 8, 1982: "Dennis Florio (675-9212, by appointment only), a consultant who supervises framing and installation of gallery shows and corporate collections, including those of the Chase Manhattan Bank, the International Paper Company and the Barbara Gladstone Gallery"

include here a close-up of my hand dialing 675-9212 on a rotary phone

why does the *Times* not specify Dennis Florio's area code?

was Florio nice to gays?

am I nice to gays?

Florio must have been nice to Neel, whose pictures he framed

and was Christopher Lazare, whom Neel painted in 1932, nice to other gays?

Neel referred to him as "queen of the homosexuals"

Lazare was a writer and a book reviewer

in *The Nation*, he reviewed a biography of Rimbaud

I recognize Lazare's nose—it is my nose, my mother's, my grandfather's

Neel depicts Lazare as an outré fop and a swank fool

but a sexually desirable fool and fop

if you are in the business of desiring fops and fools

I am in that business

his plurality (four Lazares in one small painting) demonstrates desire's rage to duplicate

the out-of-place, as a region of thought and embodiment, is hospitable to multiples, copies, series

Lazare's oddness—foppishness, nose, theatrical self-consciousness—breeds replicas

he can't help but reproduce himself, on Neel's page, so plural is his wiry yet leonine foppishness

a foppishness to which we will, resolutely, be nice

Lazare, in *The Nation*, reviewed a book called *Shining Scabbard*

define a shining scabbard

his review was titled "A Disgraced Name"

Lazare, in *The Nation*, reviewed an Ivy Compton-Burnett novel

his review was titled "Cycle of Sterility"

no one is nice in a Compton-Burnett novel

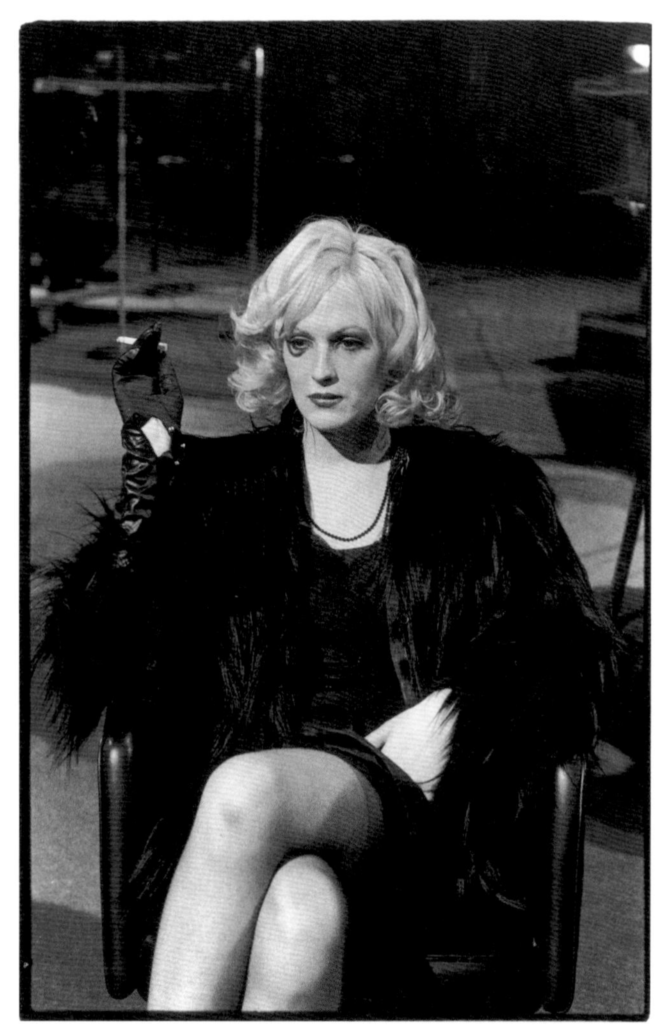

Candy Darling, 1969. Photo by Fred McDarrah

Daniel Talbot, in his memoir, *In Love with Movies*, calls Lazare "a brilliant writer whose career never took off"

are *writers whose careers never took off* nice to each other?

is it nice to say "never took off"?

Cage ends his "Lecture on Nothing" with this declaration: "All I know about method is that when I am not working I sometimes think I know something, but when I am working, it is quite clear that I know nothing"

when Neel was painting portraits she must have known nothing

because to grasp the exact proportions of a body

is not to know those proportions

but to see them

acts of recognition (I note that the chair is striped and that the man's pants are tight) needn't involve linguistically knowing anything, *pace* Wittgenstein

Hagopian's only commercially released recording, of Bartók's piano works, received not nice treatment in *The Gramophone Newsletter*: "Robert Hagopian's resources of touch and accent are not especially wide"

Hagopian's "main restriction" is "a sound-quality which all too easily becomes bulky"

my resources of touch and accent in this lecture are not especially wide

my sound-quality in this lecture all too easily becomes bulky

I once had a pair of dark blue velour pants that resemble the snug slacks that Hagopian wears in Neel's portrait

under Hagopian's butt, the chair almost disappears, so keenly does Neel allow him to approach the viewer

deep shadow flanking his right pectoral interrupts his body's continuity, like the alien visitors to abdomens and thoraxes in David Cronenberg's *Shivers*

Neel might have been thinking about nothing when she painted this unheimlich shadow and decided to make it prominent, at the risk of distracting from the painting's other elements

we need the shadow's presence to help us think about nothing, a subject as immense as the disappearance of a person I never met but am now meeting, through a painting's *Étant donnés* peephole

Hagopian's dark blue pants, tight-fitting, match or conflict with the light blue background, which doesn't render realistic space but effaces it with an allover flatness, pulsating like a sky stared at for too long

the two blues exhibit the twinship we remember from Alfred Hitchcock's *Strangers on a Train*—a sameness that leads to violent intimacy

blue and blue are not nice to each other because they need to efface their nothingness

not-niceness is the method of bulking up the effacement

Robert, in the portrait, looks at us, while the blue of his pants and the blue of the unspecific background converse with each other we are not invited to join that conversation

nothing in this portrait makes it clear that Robert Hagopian would have been nice to me

Ron Kajiwara, 1971
Oil on canvas
67 7/8 × 35 1/8 inches
172.4 × 89.2 cm

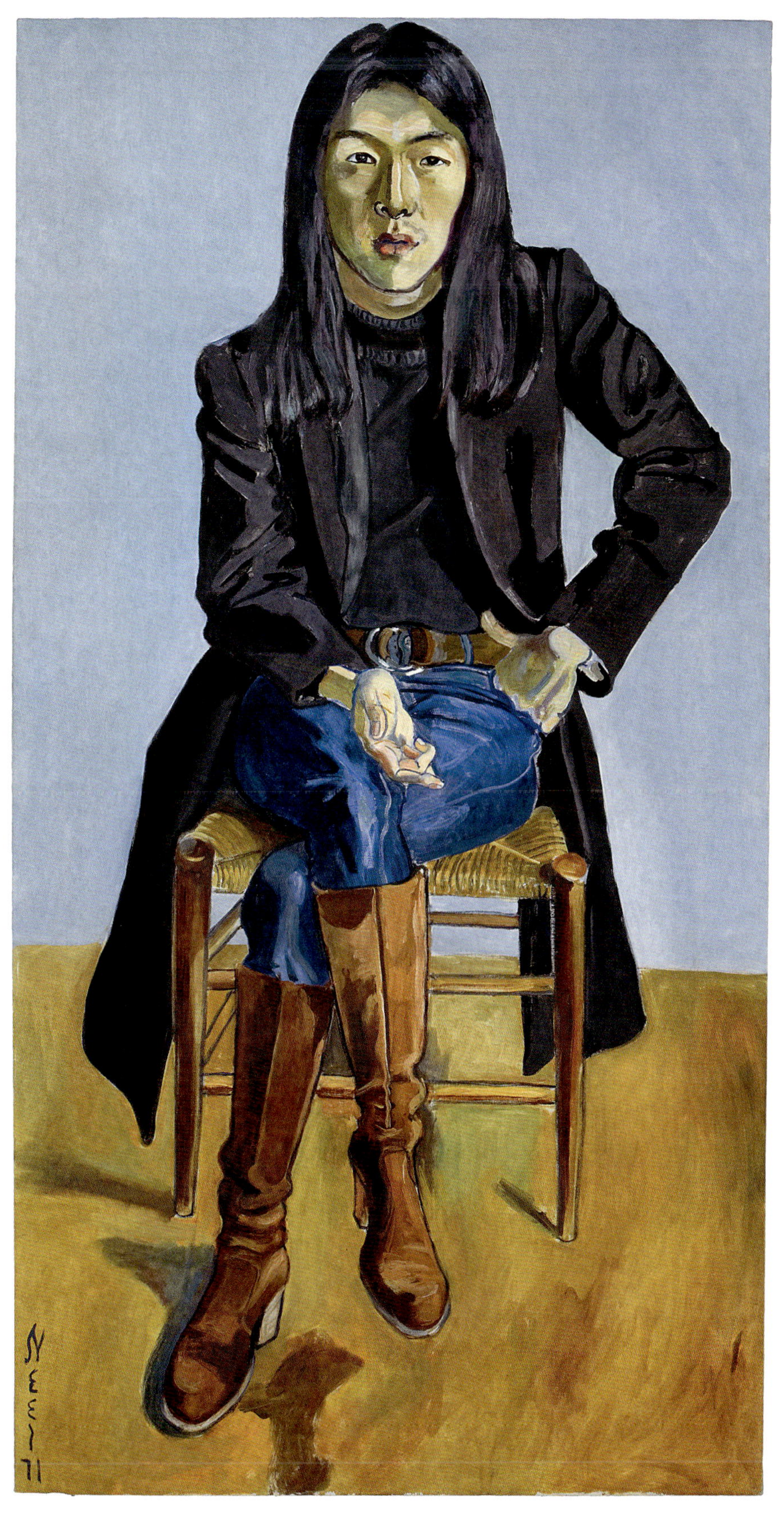

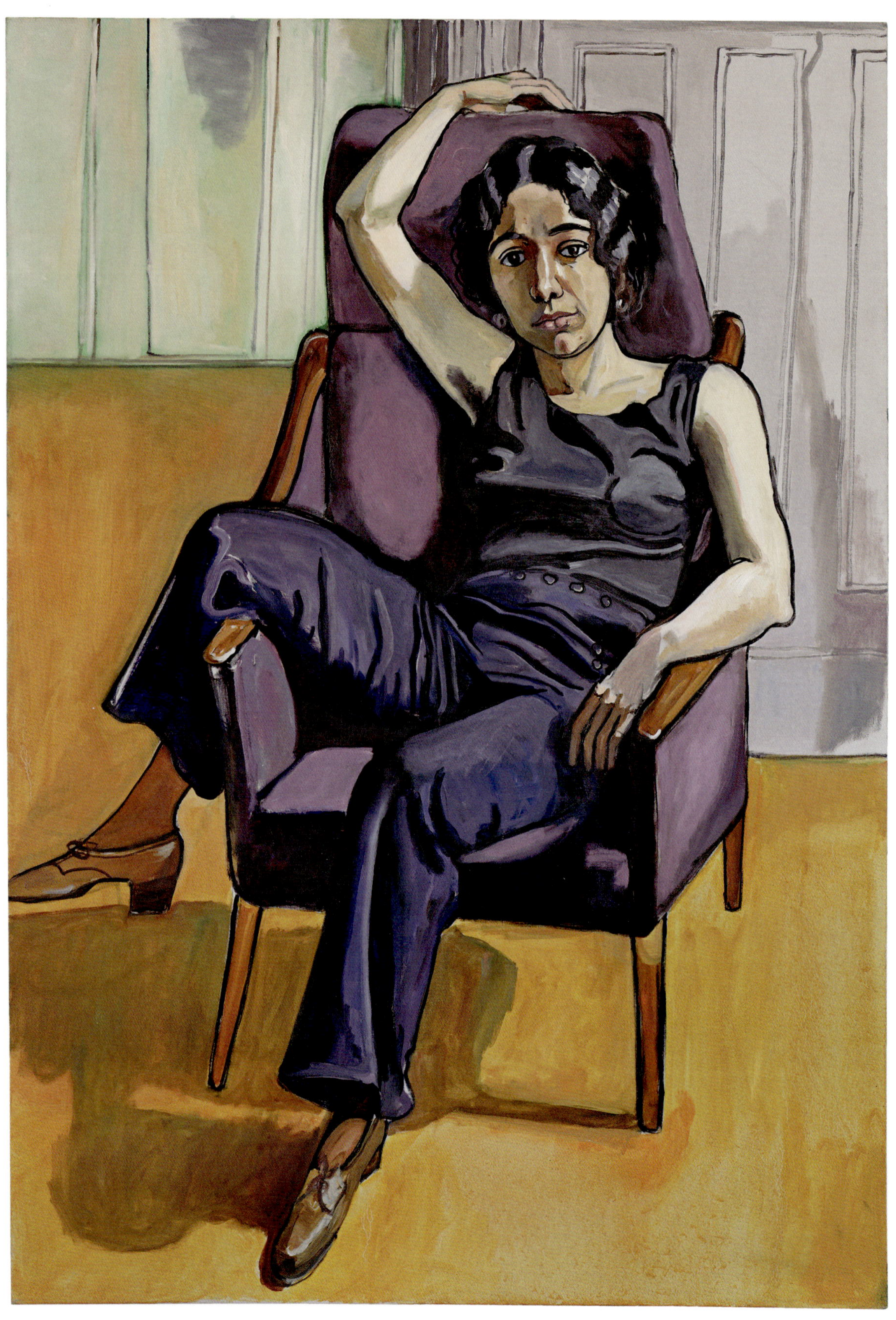

Marxist Girl (Irene Peslikis), 1972
Oil on canvas
60 × 40 inches
152.4 × 101.6 cm

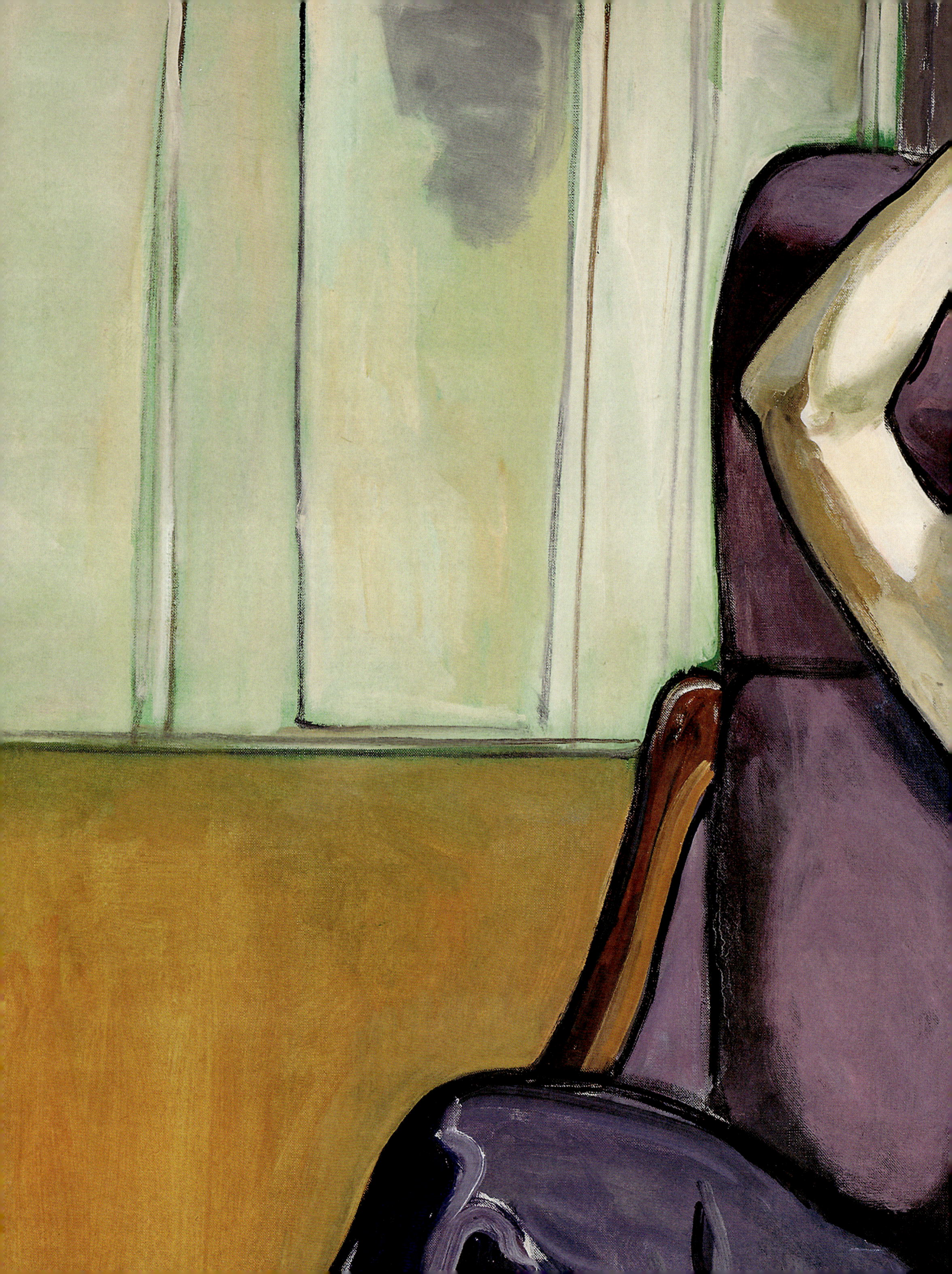

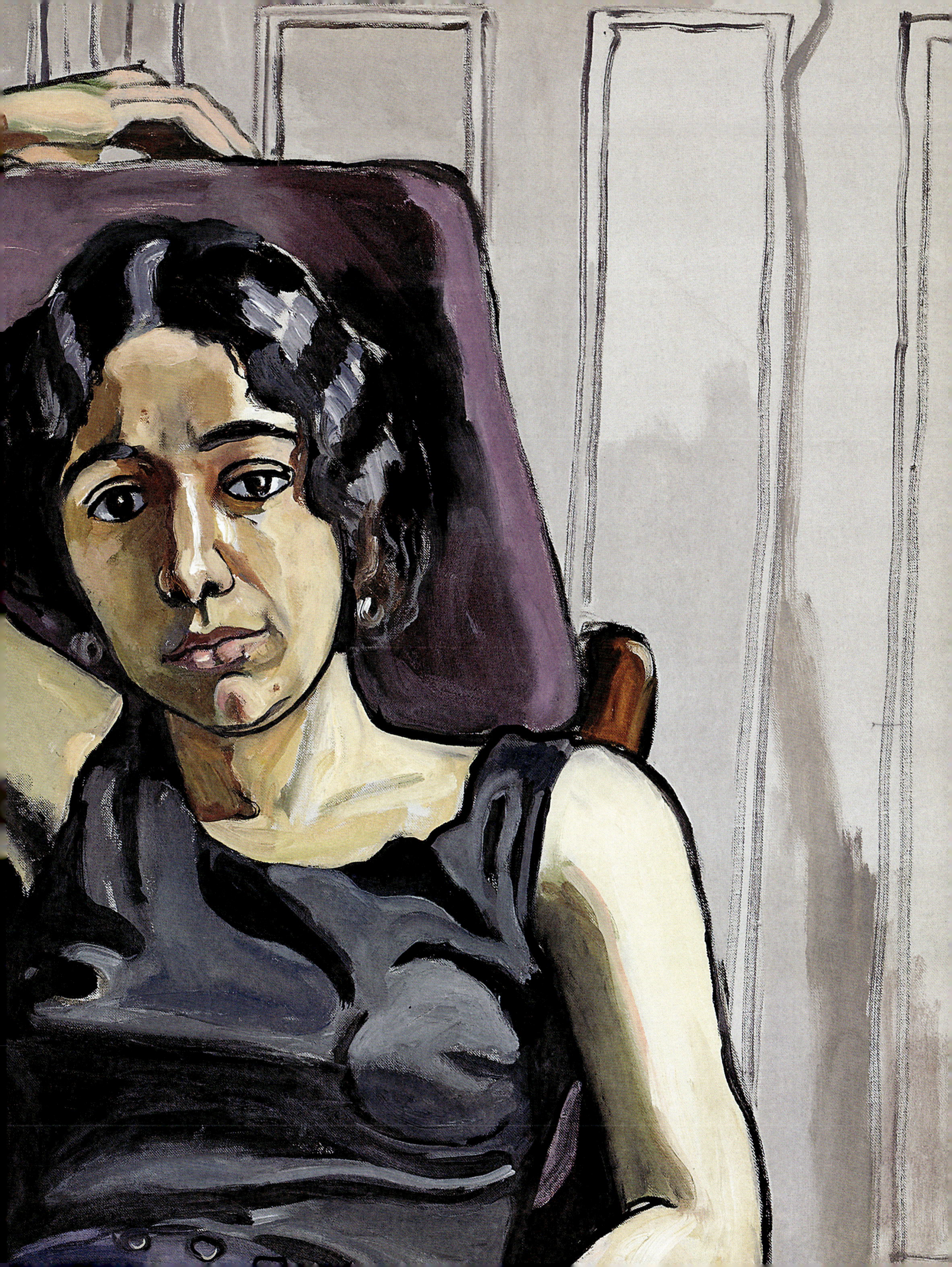

Kris Kirsten, 1971
Oil on canvas
47 7/8 × 30 inches
121.6 × 76.2 cm

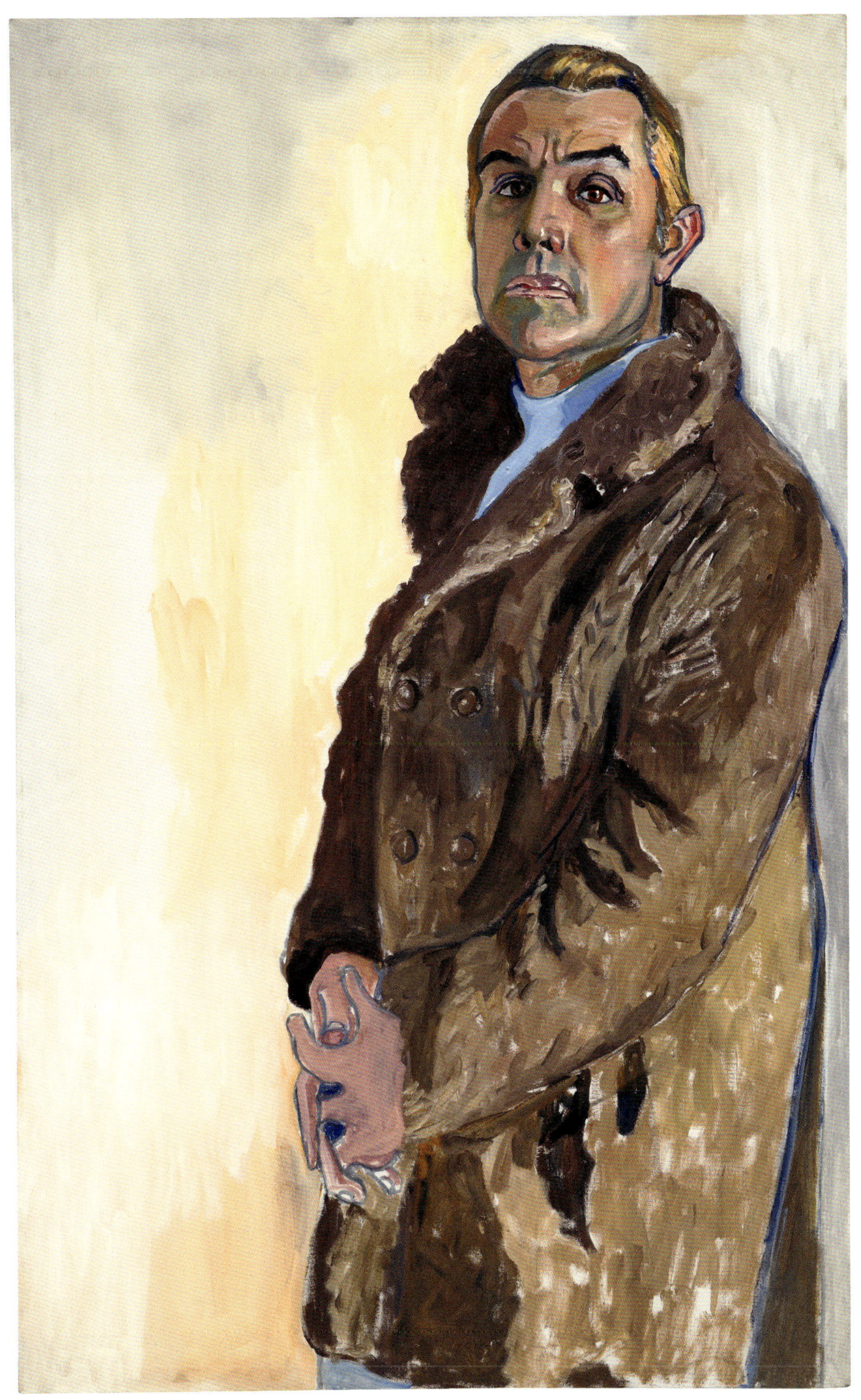

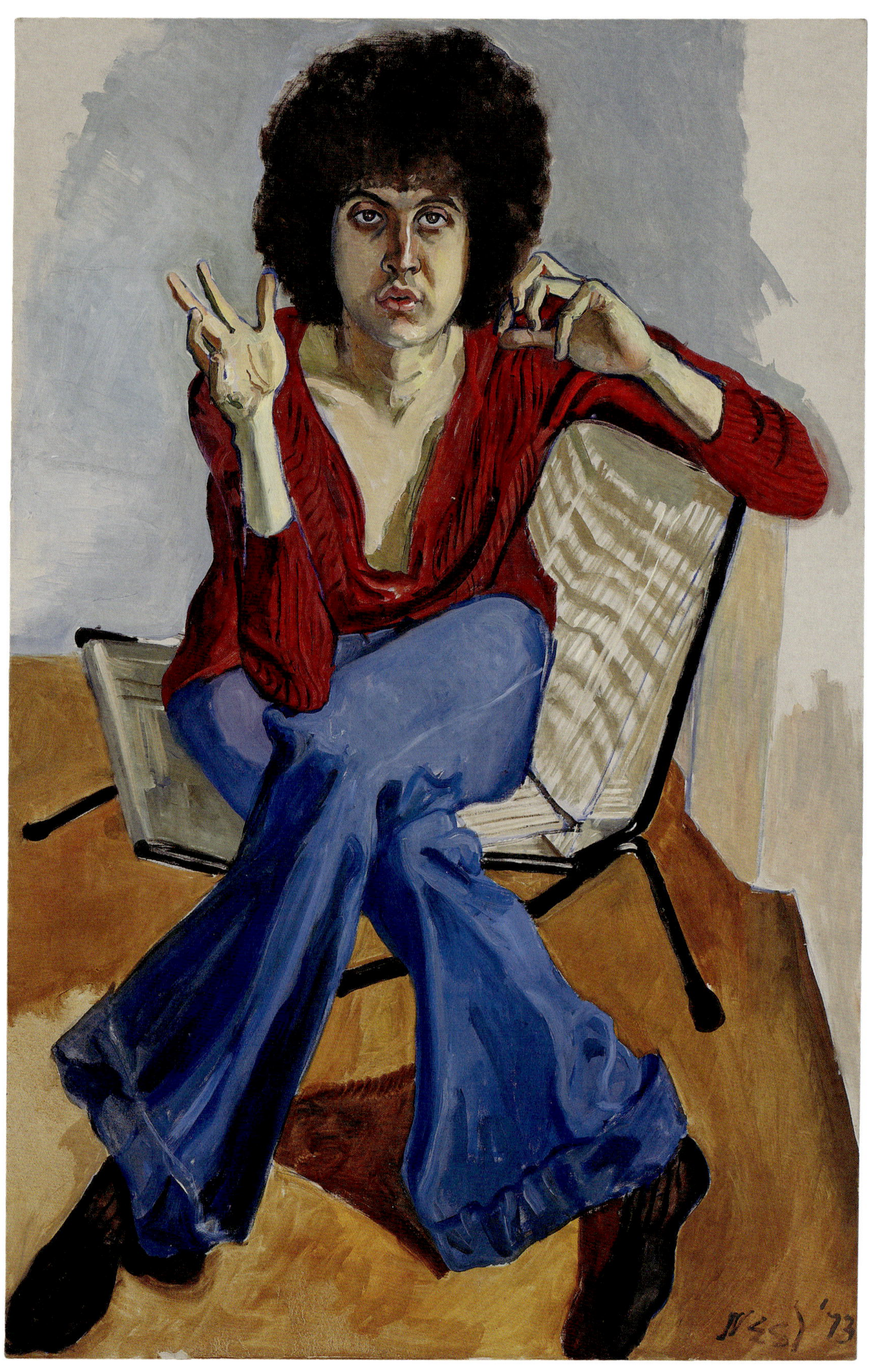

Robbie Tillotson, 1973
Oil on canvas
58 × 38 ⅛ inches
147.3 × 96.8 cm

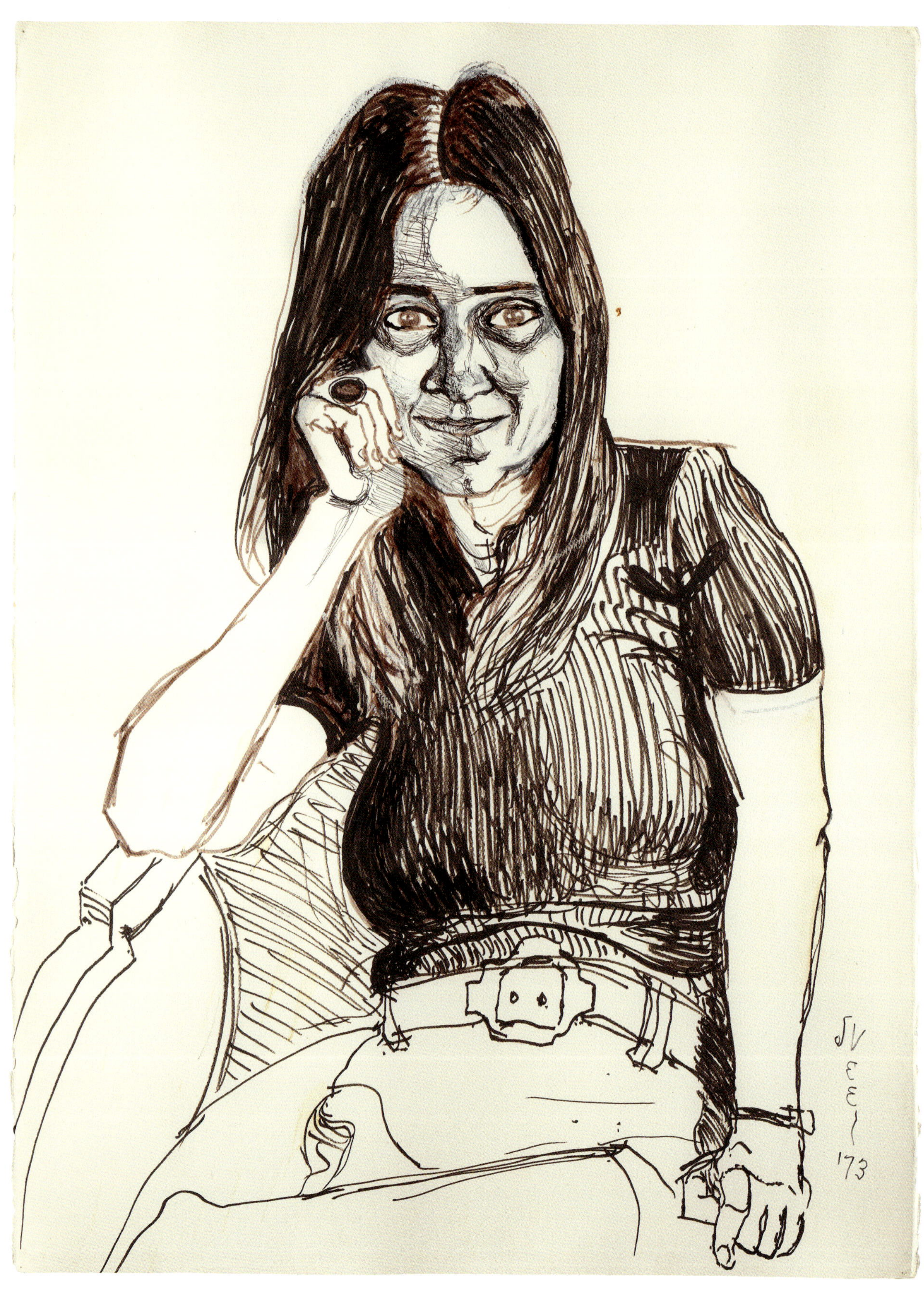
NEEL
'73

Adrienne Rich, 1973
Ink on paper
29 ¾ × 22 inches
75.6 × 55.9 cm

Jackie Curtis as a Boy, 1972
Oil on canvas
44 × 30 inches
111.8 × 76.2 cm

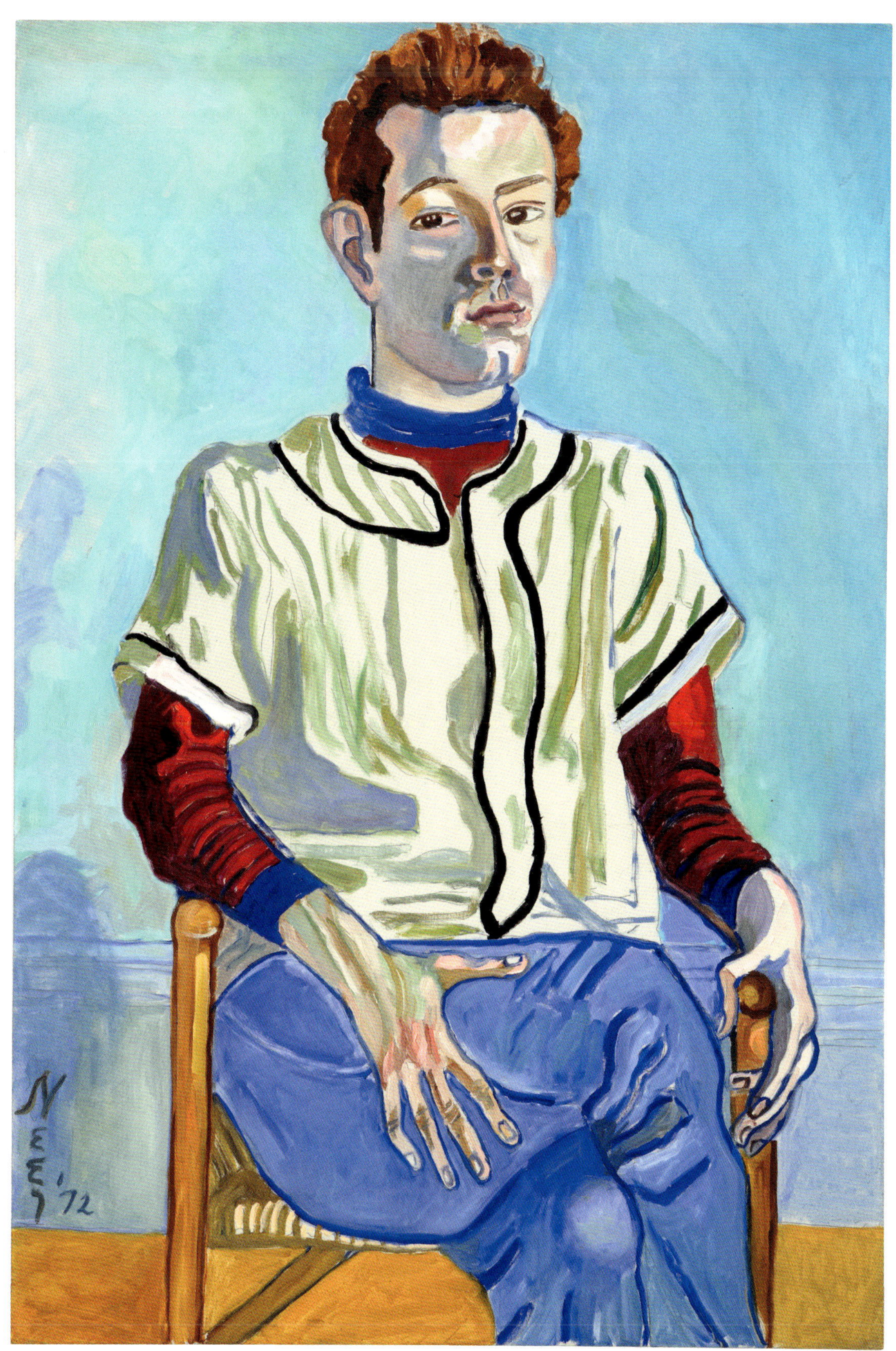
NEEL '72

Portrait of William D. Paul Jr., 1975
Oil on canvas
60 × 40 inches
152.4 × 101.6 cm

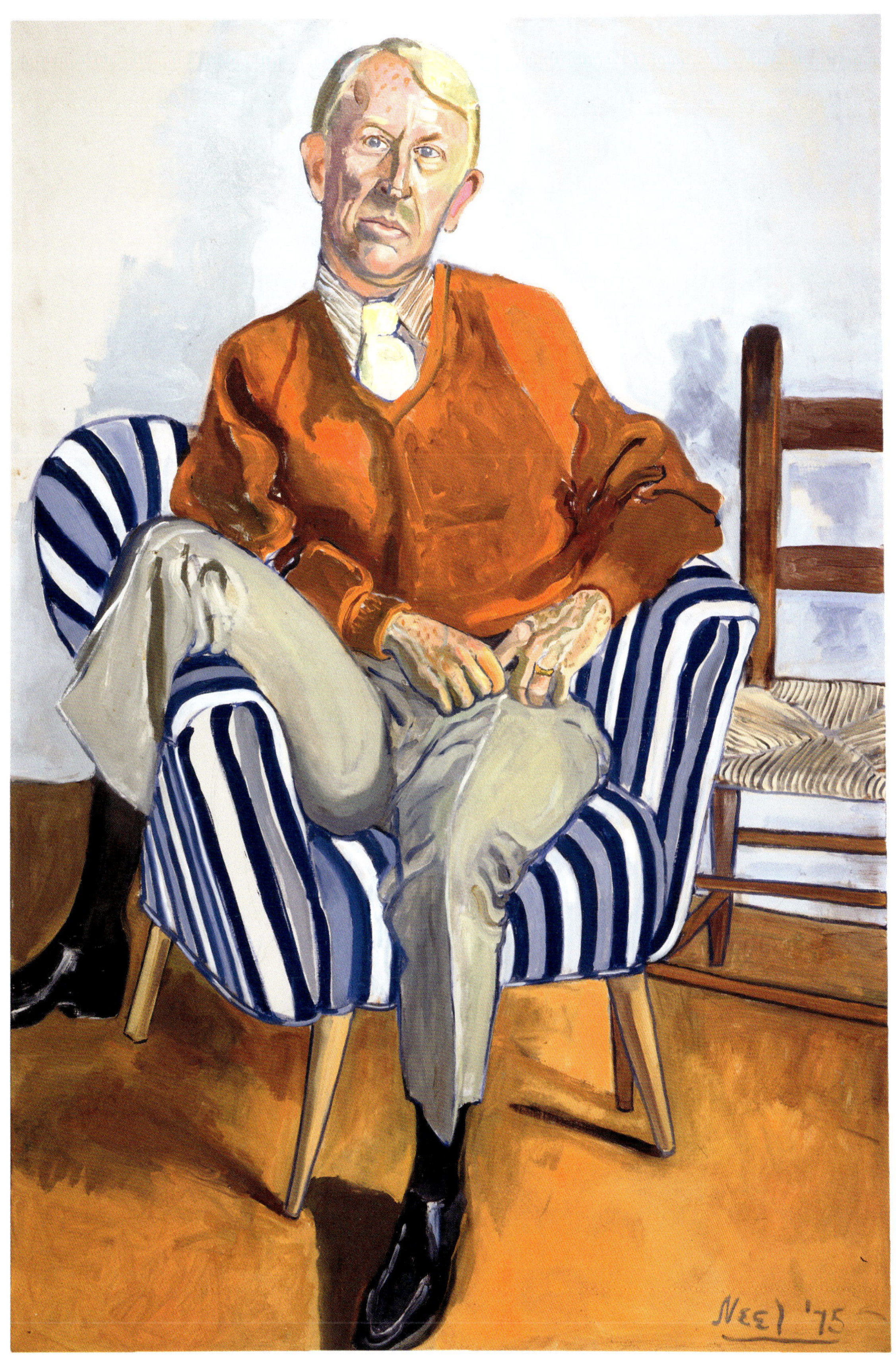
Neel '75

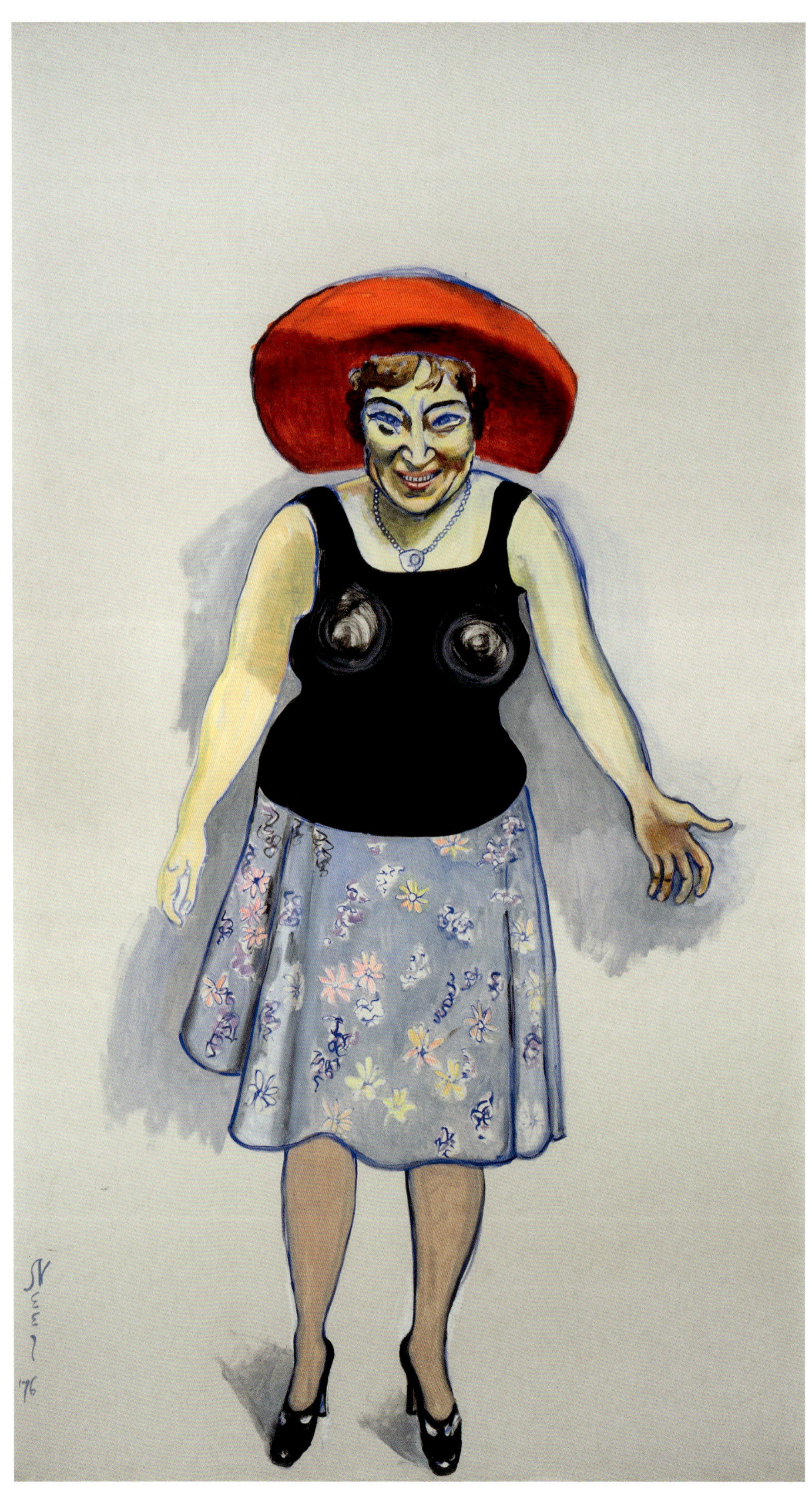

Bella Abzug, 1976
Oil on canvas
108 × 60 inches
274.3 × 152.4 cm

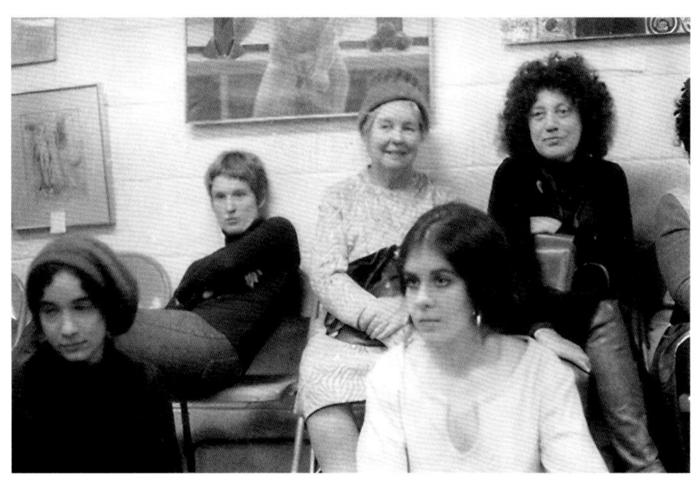

Alice Neel with Irene Peslikis (far left), Janet Sawyer, Dee Slack, and Lucia Vernarelli at a meeting of the Alliance of Figurative Artists, New York, 1971

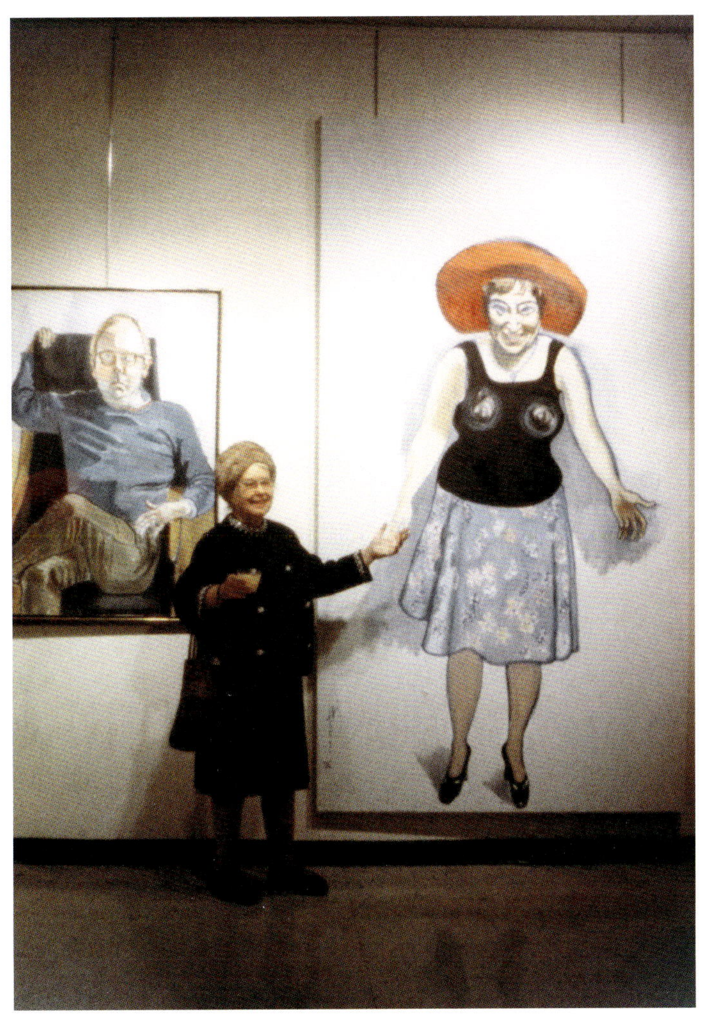

Alice Neel with her paintings *Henry Geldzahler* (1967) and *Bella Abzug* (1976) at *Women Painters and Poets: Visual Artists Coalition*, Loeb Student Center, New York University, 1977

Mary D. Garrard, 1977
Oil on canvas
33 ¼ × 29 ¼ inches
84.5 × 74.3 cm

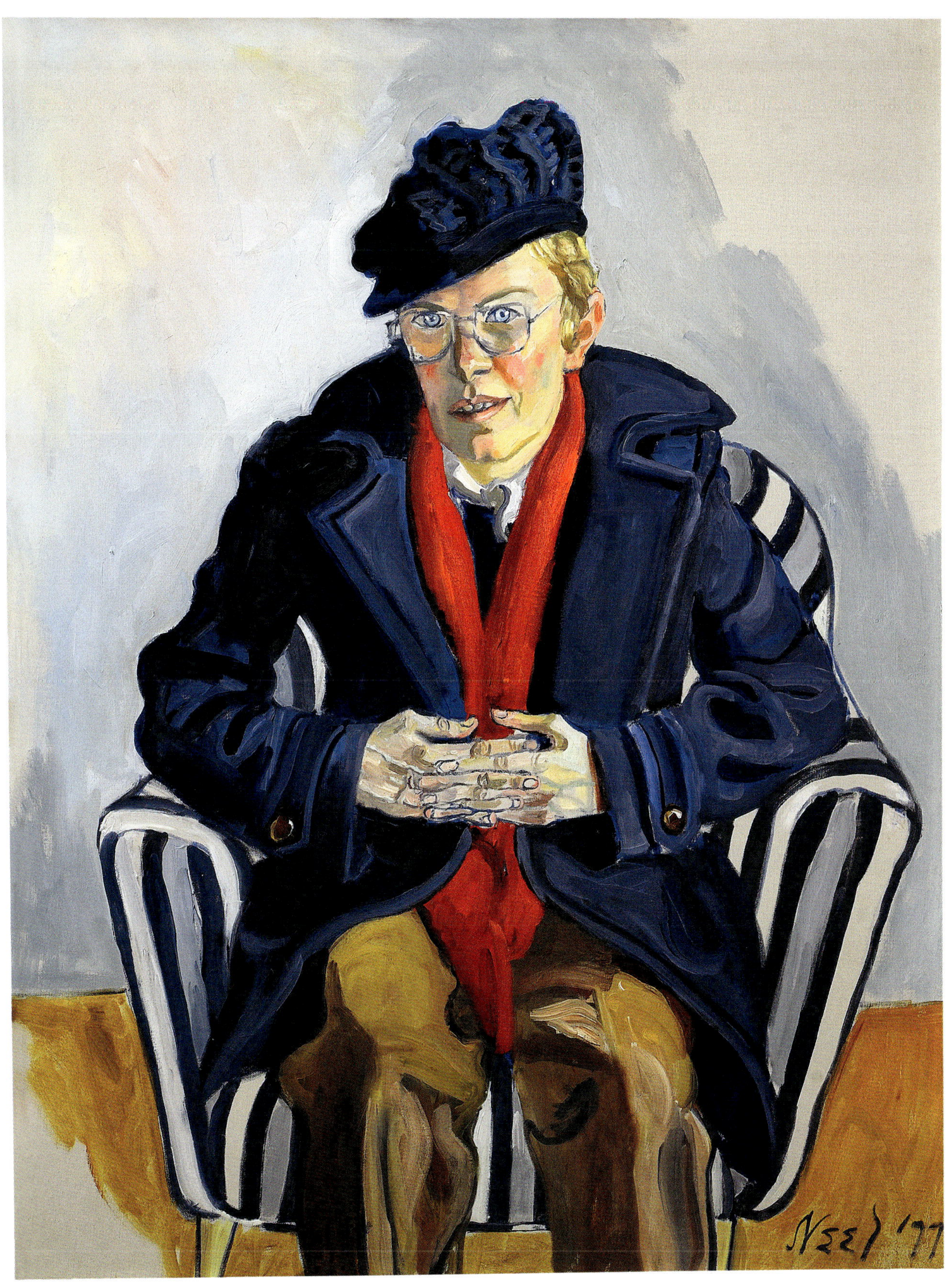

Mary Garrard, 1977
Ink and graphite on paper
30 ⅛ × 22 ½ inches
76.5 × 57.1 cm

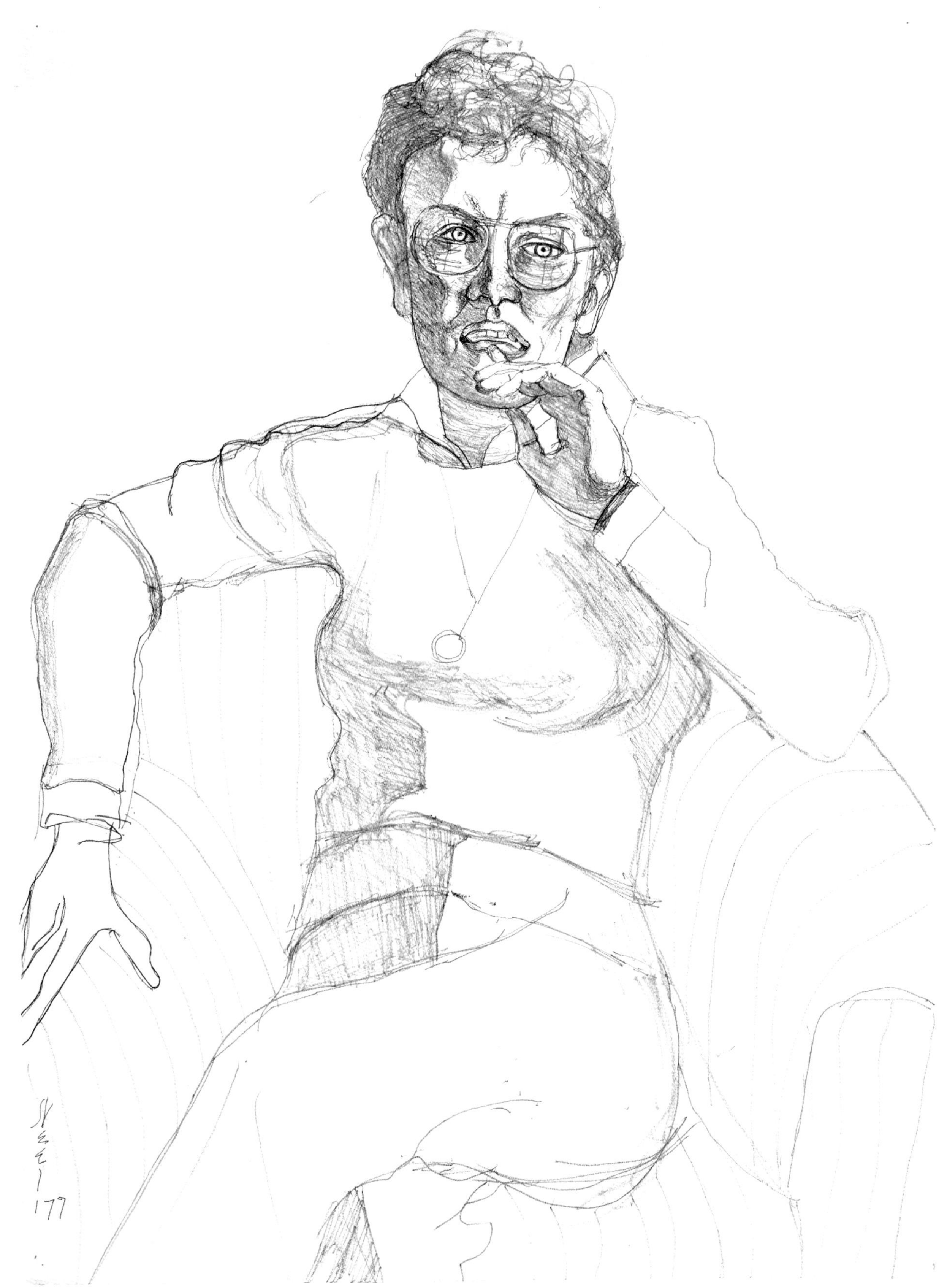

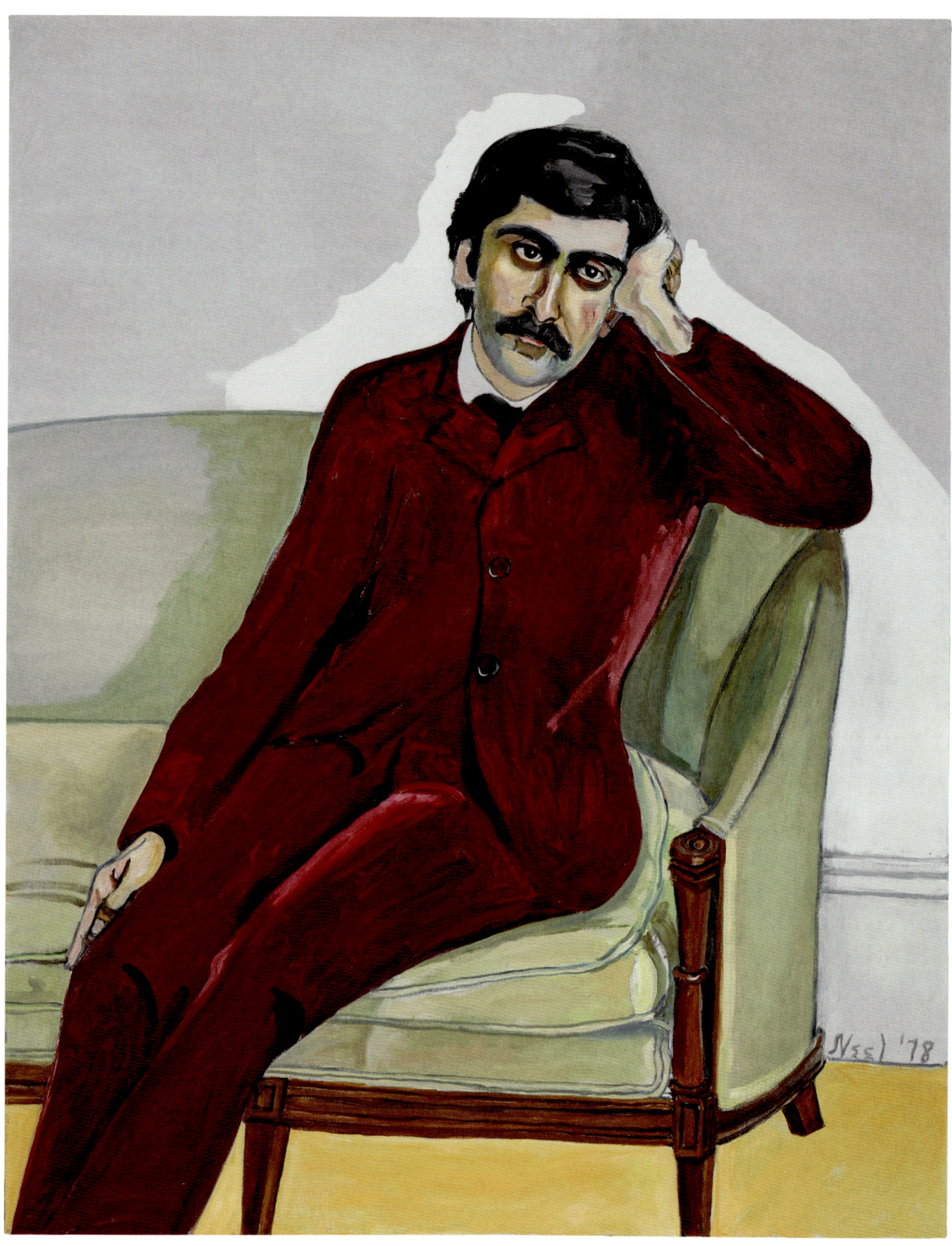
Neel '78

Dennis Florio, 1978
Oil on canvas
48 × 38 inches
121.9 × 96.5 cm

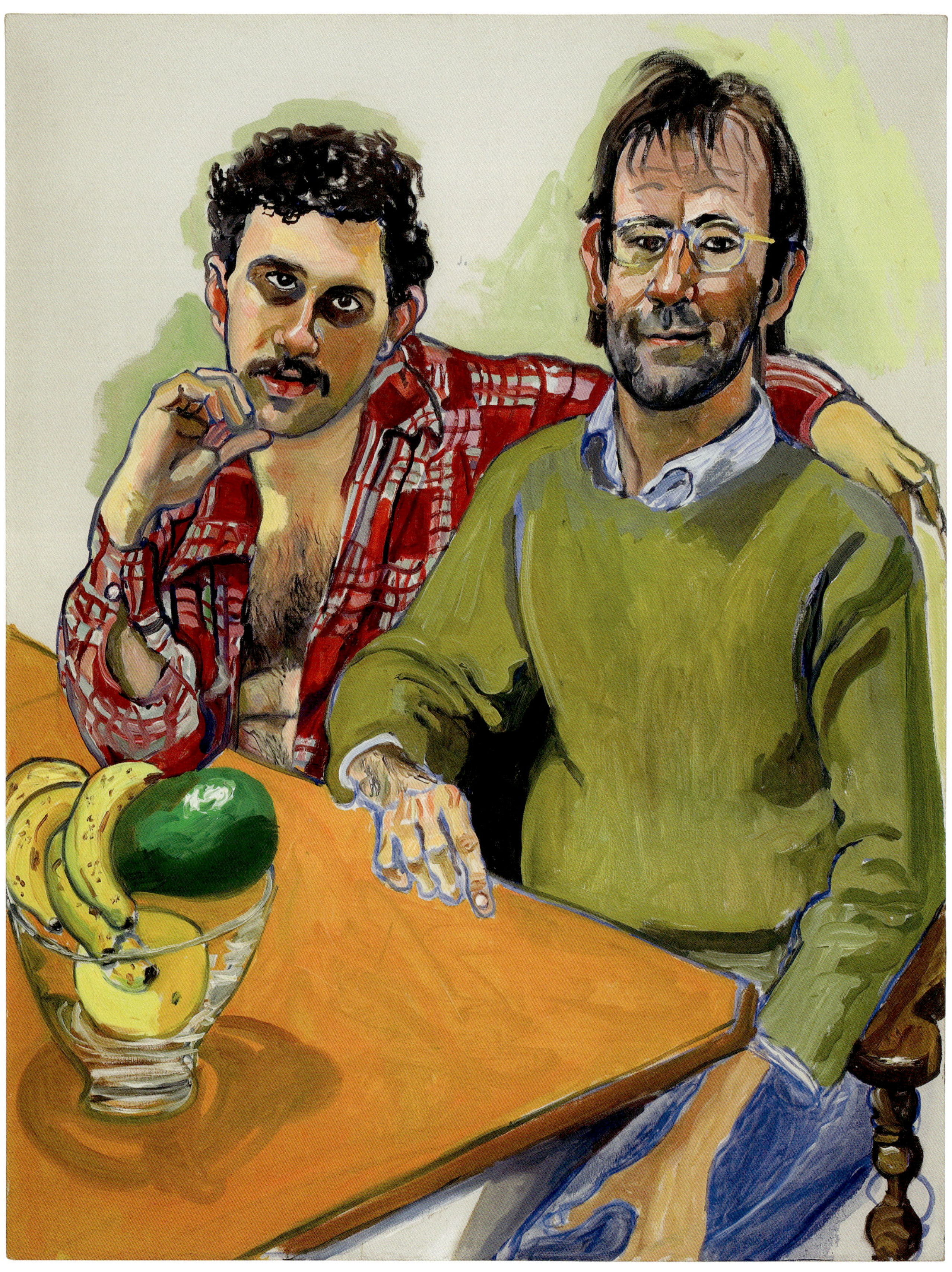

Geoffrey Hendricks and Brian, 1978
Oil on canvas
44 × 34 inches
111.8 × 86.4 cm

Cuchulain, 1979
Oil on canvas
42 × 32 inches
106.7 × 81.3 cm

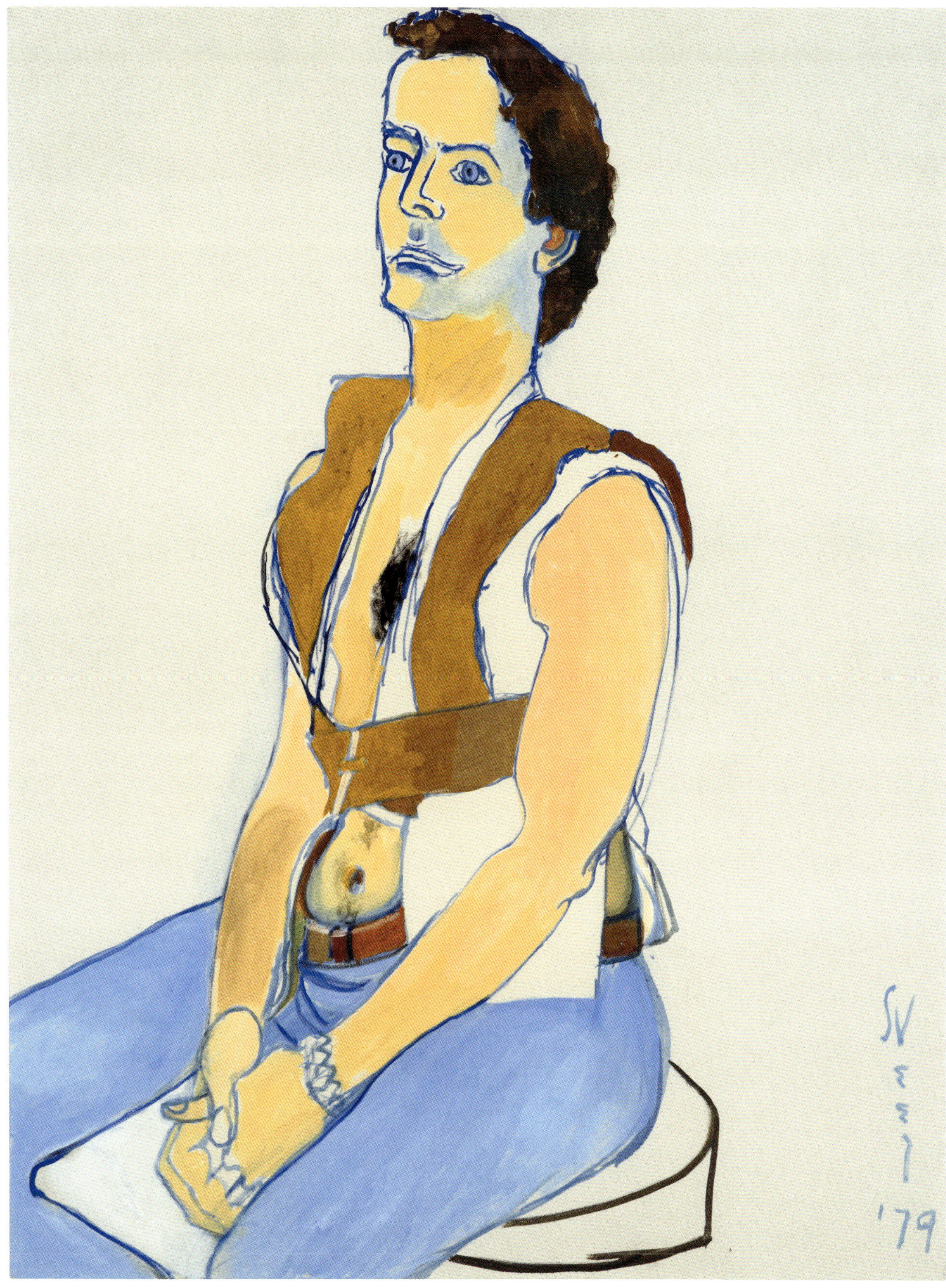
'79

John Cheim, 1979
Oil on canvas
45 ½ × 30 inches
115.6 × 76.2 cm

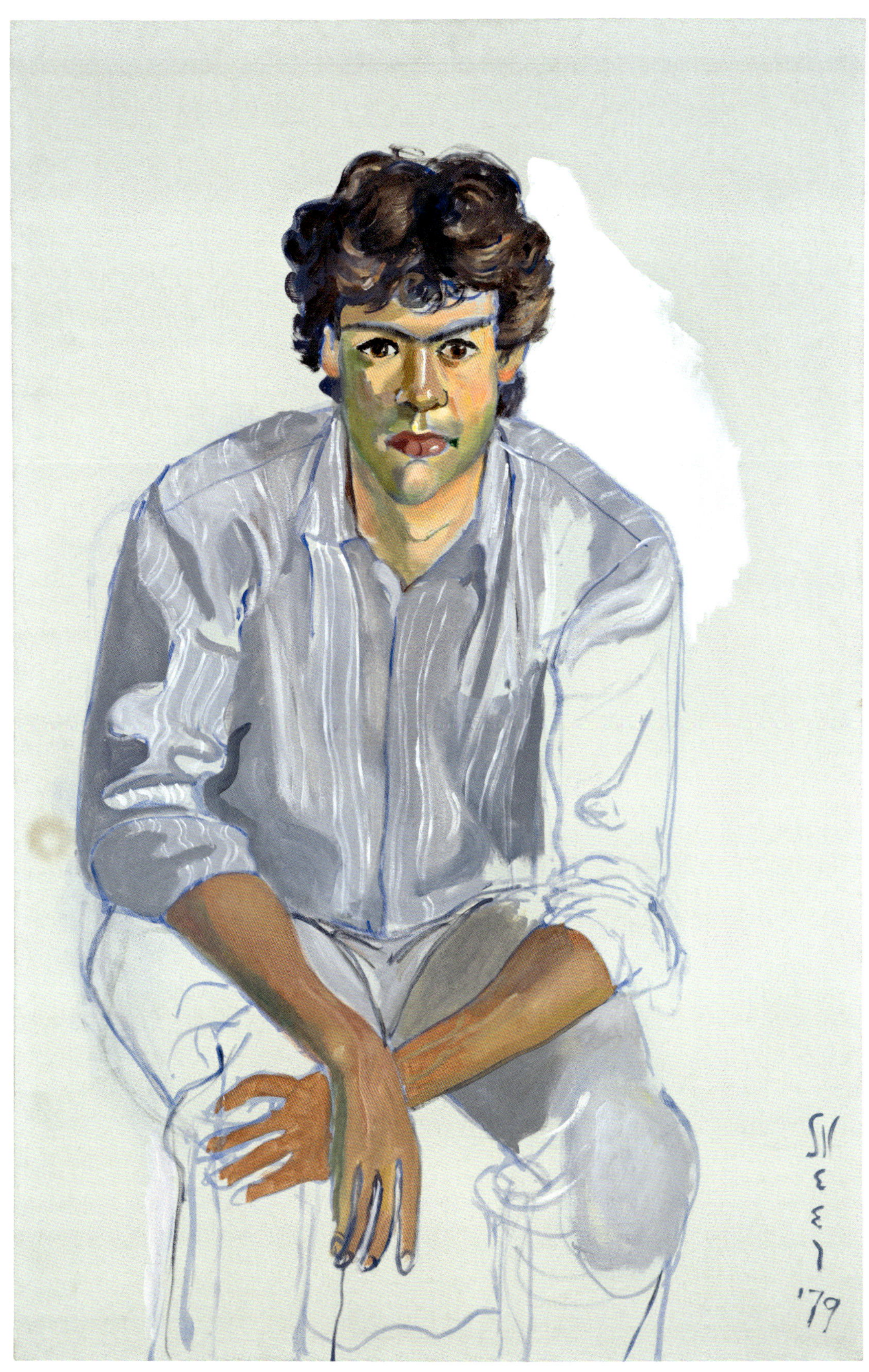

EVAN GARZA

ANNIE SPRINKLE PAINTS A PORTRAIT OF ALICE NEEL

Alice Neel's *Annie Sprinkle* (1982; p. 122) is practically naked. I don't mean the work's subject, the ecofeminist performance artist, porn pioneer, and queer sexual icon, who is seductively clad in leather lingerie and vintage pumps as tall as buildings. I mean that the painting itself, its compositional body, is so bare it may as well be nude. Within Alice Neel's decades-long oeuvre, this provocative late-career portrait—one of the artist's last before her death—is perhaps her most revealing for its remarkable restraint.

In Neel's oil paintings there's often some hint about the setting of her sitters—a familiar chair, the color of an adjacent wall, a garden, an entire room—which, in a way, is itself also portraitized in the final work. Many of Neel's paintings after 1962, the year she moved to her final New York apartment on the Upper West Side,[1] reveal a cast of furniture characters that make repeated appearances in her work: a plush mustard chair with a ruffled skirt, wooden armchairs with green upholstery, a semicircular blue-and-white-striped reading chair, a myriad of sofas, and a modest wood and woven seagrass dining chair, among many others. Depicted over time, they become almost like regulars at a Manhattan bar, each with their own personality, drawing other characters into their orbit and, eventually, their seats.

However, in the portrait of Sprinkle we find practically nothing in the way of furniture: some flecks of muted, ruddy orange, a few faint blue lines like the ghost of a stool, and the position of Sprinkle's body respective to the white negative space around her. This wasn't Neel's first skin pic; she painted a nude self-portrait two years prior at the age of eighty. Nor was this the first time the artist deployed this degree of compositional restraint—there's her 1970 shirtless portrait of Andy Warhol or an airy blue-and-white picture of John Cheim, painted in 1979, showing him seated with no sign of a chair (p. 117), as well as several other works with ample negative space. What is remarkable here, when compared to Neel's other compositionally "bare" works, is the captivating power that Sprinkle and her sexually charged body have over the viewer. In that apartment in 1982, that viewer was Neel.

"It's really nice to be seen and studied. It's erotic, frankly, to be seen," Sprinkle says of both her experience being painted by Neel and the eyes of viewers on her painted body. On a recent summery San Francisco afternoon, she told me the story of sitting for Neel. "It was a sexy experience. Creativity and sexuality are very linked, as queers know pretty well. . . . I had that leather outfit made, and the bust was totally cut out and the crotch. I brought a suitcase full of stuff for Alice to pick from, and she picked that. I had my labia pierced right around then, and I showed it to her. I wasn't shy. She seemed very queer to me—her curiosity. We were pretty flirty, but I was flirty with everybody back then."[2]

Sprinkle describes Neel as a daring artist and one who dared to paint herself naked. She recognized that, like her, Neel was a provocateur. For the length of Neel's career, it was groundbreaking for a mature woman to be an artist, much less one who moved uptown when the entire art world was downtown. In 1982, Sprinkle was working as a pro dom in New York, making porn, and working at the Hellfire Club. She was one of only three women allowed at Mineshaft, a men's members-only BDSM leather bar and gay sex club in the Meatpacking District. At the time, a painting of a porn star in fetish gear might have seemed provocative to the straight world, but perhaps not to Neel, who devoted so much of her practice and, ultimately, her life to making pictures of sexual and gender minorities. As Hilton Als has noted, Neel was "attracted to a world of difference,"[3] and Sprinkle was a world unto herself. Neel and Sprinkle were pioneers. Pushing boundaries was the point for both women.

Sprinkle's labia had recently been pierced by Fakir Musafar, whom she describes as "the father of modern-day body piercing," and whose foreskin she had recently pierced herself.[4] In Neel's portrait, Sprinkle's labia ring hangs between her open legs like the anthesis of a flower bud expanding and expressing itself. There's a palpable sense of pride in her posture and composure as she shares her vulva and ample breasts, or "the girls," as she calls them. A feather comb sits atop her wavy red hair, delicately teasing the negative space around her. Sprinkle's impossibly tall heels, a pair of black leather pumps from the 1940s fetish world, were a gift from Musafar, who collected vintage sex gear and whose legendary body-piercing practice inspired greats like Ron Athey.[5]

In 1982, Sprinkle had not yet fully blossomed as the performance artist and queer icon she would soon become. "At that point with Alice, I was definitely this kinky porn-star prostitute friend," Sprinkle explains. "The term 'sex worker' didn't exist. . . . She was a provocateur herself, the amount of queer portraits she did was provocative for a straight lady. Though I don't know how straight she was. I wouldn't be surprised if she'd had women lovers. She was adventurous. In 1982, I was barely queer. I mean I was always queer because I never fit in the norm. I had sex with women, but I had sex with all kinds of people. I don't know that I was out as queer, but I certainly *was* queer and certainly became a hundred percent queer. Of course, we're ecosexuals now, but that's another story."[6]

Annie met Alice through their mutual friend and gay fine-art framer to the stars, Dennis Florio, whom Neel painted in 1978. In his portrait, Florio dons a deep cabernet-red suit atop the artist's living room sofa, a simple green settee (p. 110). With his arm perched on the couch he rests his temple in the palm of his hand as if paused in a moment of reflection or engaged with Neel in conversation. Unlike Sprinkle's portrait, Florio's is one of incredible modesty. His jacket is buttoned all the way up to his necktie, and the only visible skin in the picture belongs to his hands and the flush contrast of his cheeks. What's more, the details of the room are captured in full, from the yellow floor to the molding of the baseboard. No compositional detail is left to the imagination. By contrast, Neel's picture of Sprinkle is a kind of tease: big tits and leather, but no clues about the room. The fact that the viewer has to fill in the blanks is, in part, what makes the work such a knockout.

"When she stopped painting, Alice said, 'I think it's done,'" Sprinkle explains. "I came over to see the work and I said, 'Oh, aren't you going to paint the chair in?' and she said, 'No, I think it's done.' She was very fascinated with the piercing and the boobage and really interested in the body. . . . The painting celebrates the erotic body."[7]

Neel's choice to cut the recurring cast of interior characters arguably provided Sprinkle with her first one-woman show, a feat she would come to achieve regularly by the end of the decade. The method of isolating the figure in the foreground while the setting retreats or is absent entirely is one Neel used several times in her work. But here, her focus on the openness of Sprinkle's body in the painting and the choice to exclude any discernible surrounding details offer both women a particularly acute power. For Sprinkle, that authority is generated by the sheer presence of her body and the command she demands softly, intimately, and intensely while remaining excited, curious, and vulnerable, conditions articulated perfectly in her face. Neel's power was her masterful skill as a painter to convey so much intimacy, so much intensity, with so little paint. Her power was also her heroic choice to produce so many queer portraits.

This is a picture of a woman seeing, studying, and capturing the power of another woman—provocateur to provocateur. In that sense, the work is also a kind of self-portrait, a conduit for their shared and respective strength, both as artists and as women, with Sprinkle in command of attention. Seated here, captivating and alluring, inviting—in control—Sprinkle and her body *dominate* the painting and the viewer's eye. That power is given to her by Neel. In sitting for the artist, Sprinkle took direction instead of giving orders. Alice Neel domming the dom at the age of eighty-two. Now that's power.

Notes

1 Rennie McDougall, "Alice Neel's Apartment Is Still a Portrait of the Artist at Work," *T: The New York Times Style Magazine* (September 12, 2021), p. 62.

2 Annie Sprinkle, conversation with the author, San Francisco, August 27, 2023.

3 Hilton Als, press release for *Alice Neel, Uptown*, David Zwirner, New York, 2017, p. 2.

4 Annie Sprinkle, "Fakir Musafar (1930–2018)," *Artforum* (August 24, 2018), accessed online.

5 Sprinkle, "Fakir Musafar (1930–2018)."

6 Sprinkle, conversation with the author, August 27, 2023.

7 Sprinkle, conversation with the author, August 27, 2023.

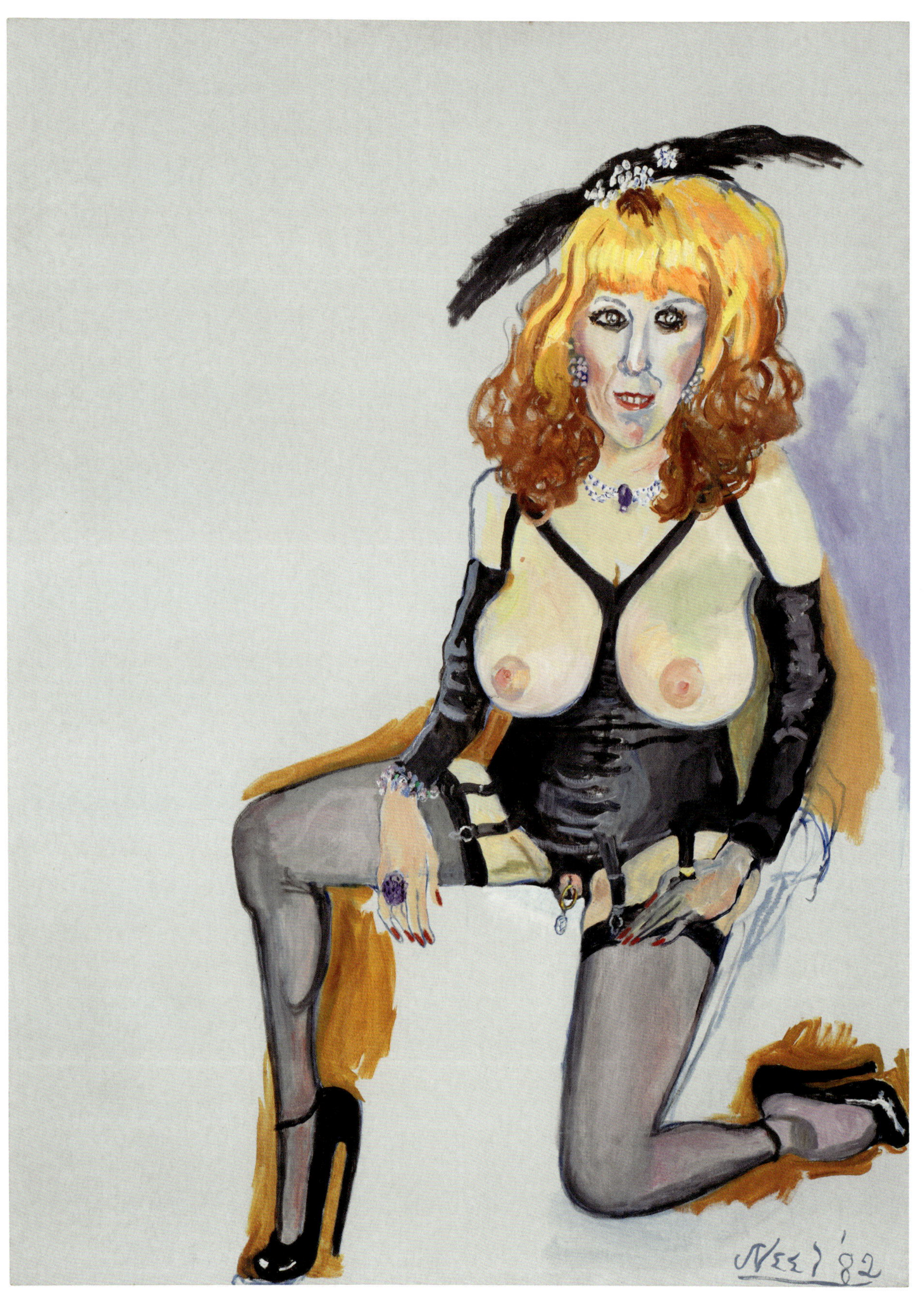
Neel '82

Annie Sprinkle, 1982
Oil on canvas
60 ⅞ × 44 ⅛ inches
154.6 × 112.1 cm

Mayor Koch, 1981
Oil on canvas
65 ¾ × 40 inches
167 × 101.6 cm

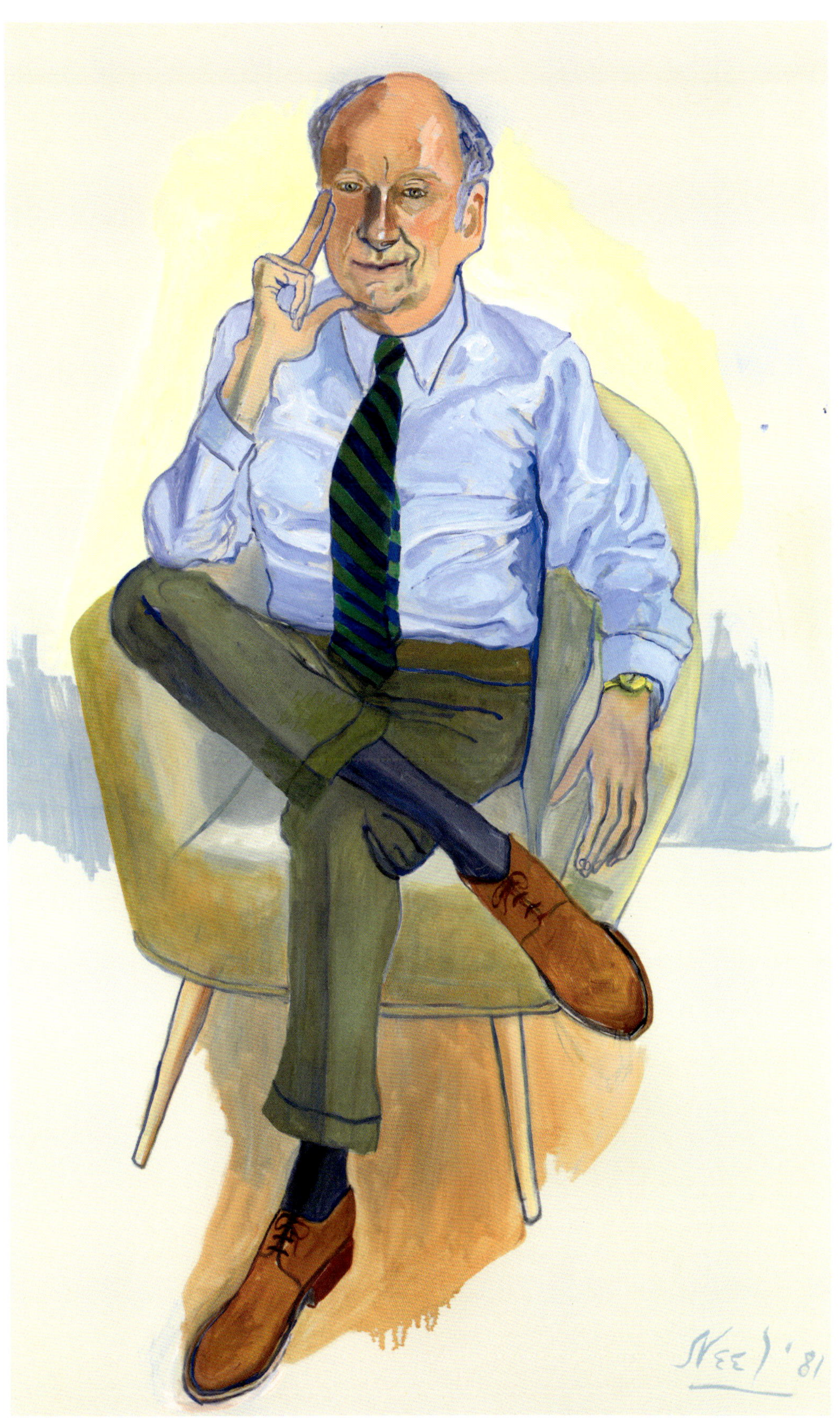
NEEL '81

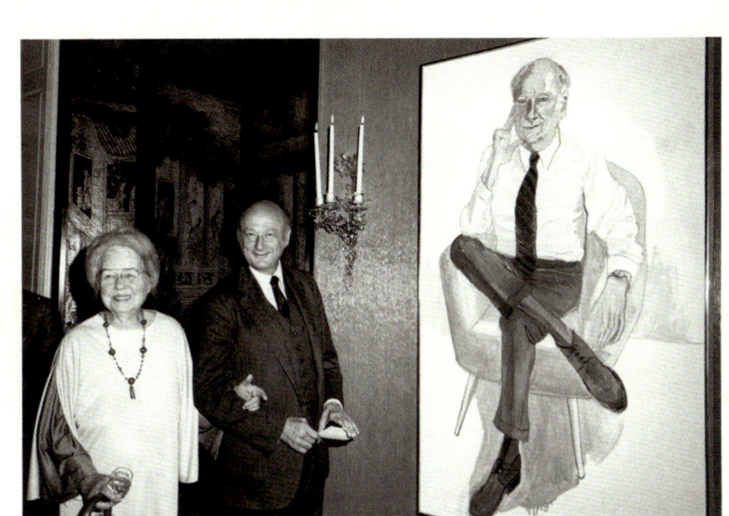

Alice Neel with Mayor Ed Koch and his portrait, Gracie Mansion, New York, 1982

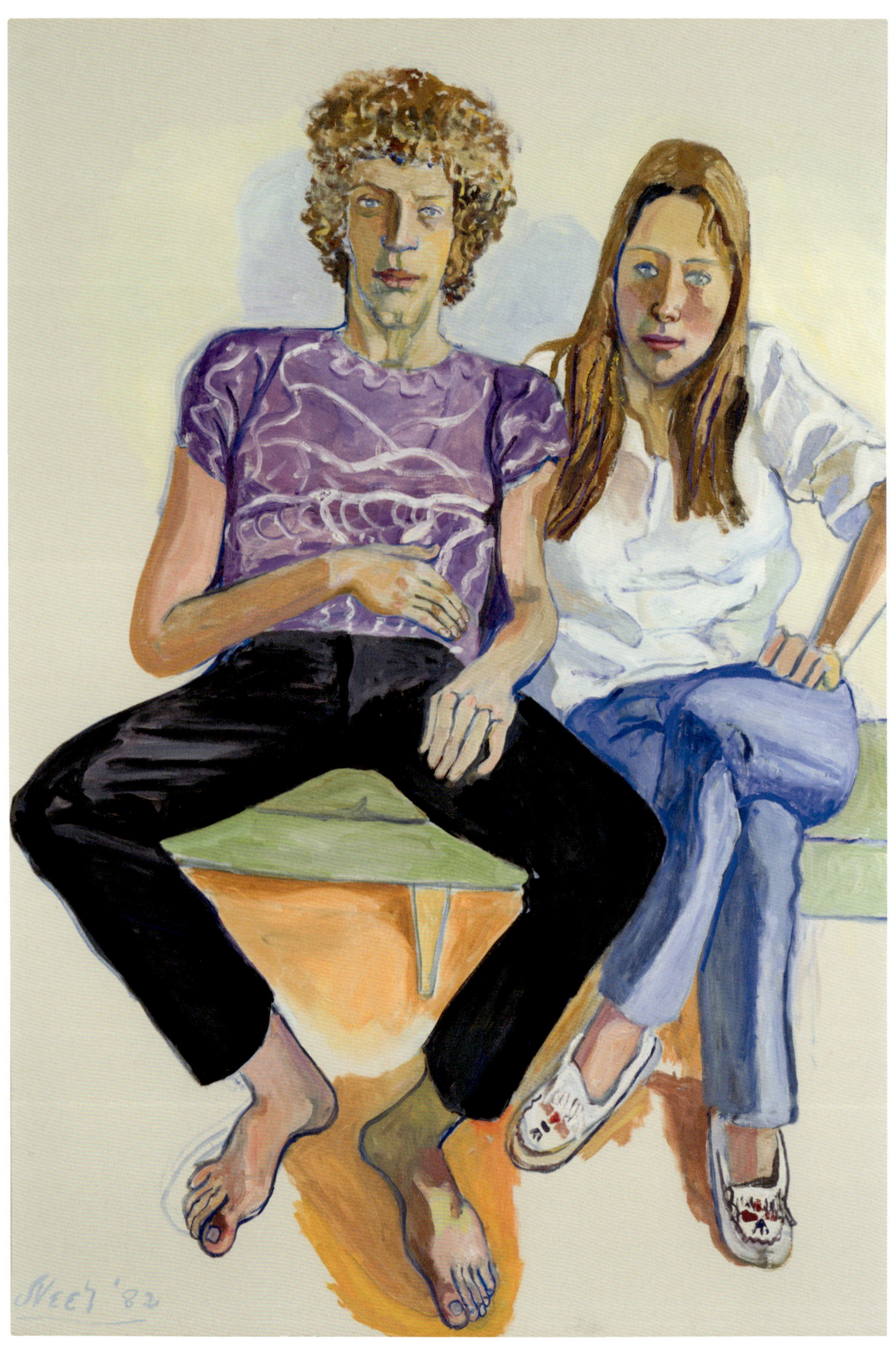
Neel '82

David and Catherine Saalfield, 1982
Oil on canvas
55 × 40 inches
139.7 × 101.6 cm

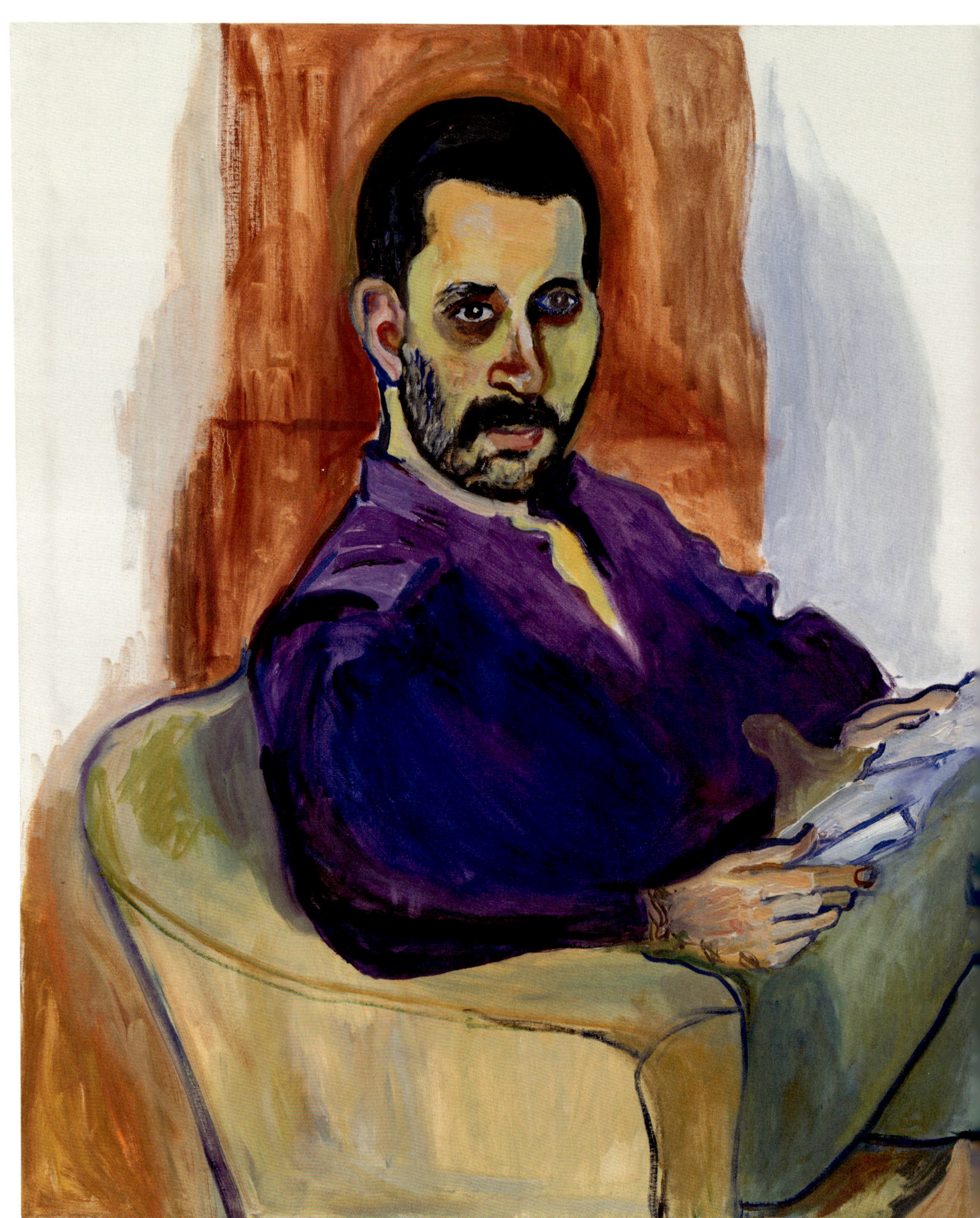

Brian Buczak, 1983
Oil on canvas
36 × 48 inches
91.4 × 121.9 cm

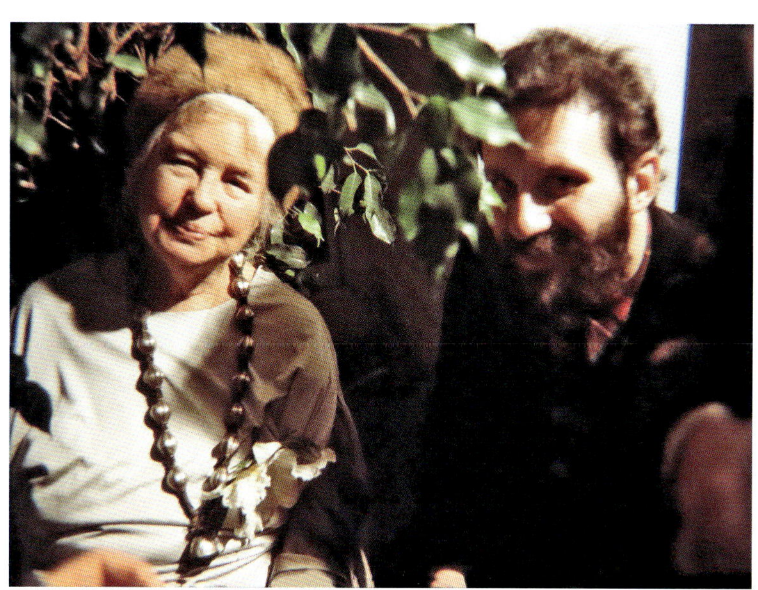

Alice Neel and Brian Buczak celebrating Neel's eightieth birthday, 1980

ALEX FIALHO

VANTAGE POINTS: ON ALICE NEEL AND AIDS

Alice Neel's portraits of people are also a portrait of their time. Indeed, many of the paintings brought together in *At Home: Alice Neel in the Queer World* are shadowed by the AIDS pandemic, as several of the sitters Neel depicted later passed from AIDS-related complications. As curator Randall Griffey writes, "While [Neel] died without realizing as much, her portraits of the 1970s recorded a generation of young gay men just before it would be devastated by disease. In addition to Brian Buczak, AIDS would claim several of Neel's sitters, including Dennis Florio, Roger Jacoby, Ron Kajiwara, Robbie Tillotson, and Ritta Redd."[1] By focusing on two portraits and people Neel painted in the early 1980s—artist Brian Buczak and New York City mayor Ed Koch—this essay traces the impact of the AIDS pandemic through these two men's differing positions in relationship to the disease. Neel's paintings open onto AIDS-related narratives that intersect but do not cohere, just as Buczak and Koch saw and experienced the pandemic and New York City from varying vantage points.

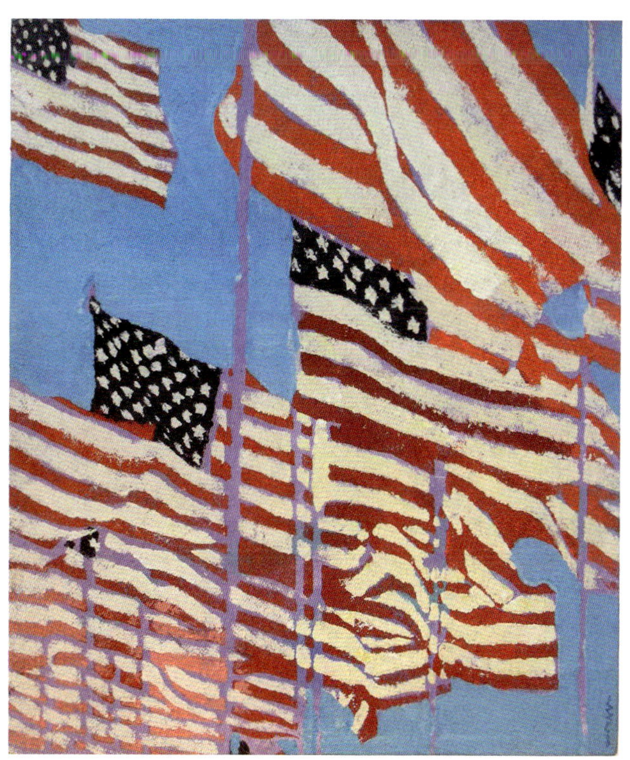

Brian Buczak, *Flags I*, 1986. Acrylic on canvas, 15 × 13 inches (38.1 × 33 cm)

Neel's painting *Brian Buczak* (pp. 130–131) is a record of two artists toward the end of their lives. Neel made this portrait of Buczak in 1983, a year before she died at age eighty-four from colon cancer, and four years before he died at age thirty-two from AIDS-related complications. Neel's painting is a tender depiction of Buczak, seated in a chair with an open book, wearing a purple long-sleeve shirt, yellow undershirt, and green pants.[2] A few oddities stand out. As is sometimes the case in Neel's paintings, one area of the figure's body appears to be scaled larger than another: Buczak's left leg is cropped at the shin and the heel of his right foot looks as if it was made to barely fit into the frame, contributing to the impression that his crossed legs are disproportionate to his larger torso and head. Also, Buczak's arms, too short for his body, appear to merge into his shirt and the book he holds. (I wonder, what was he reading?) Neel seems to be rendering Buczak from multiple vantage points—above, below, off to the side—resulting in these irresolvable visual details. Adding to the sense of spatial dislocation, she portrays Buczak floating in the foreground, without a focal point or a definitive horizon line in the indistinguishable background, disregarding the precision of linear one-point perspective for an imbalanced and evocative effect. In perspectival terms, Neel's paintings are definitively not straight; one might even say that they are queer.

This skewed perspective in Neel's paintings can leave the viewer feeling a little off-kilter, albeit intentionally so. It's difficult to know where Neel stood in relation to her sitter; as a result, the viewer has trouble resolving where they stand relative to the depicted body. Whereas linear perspective emanates from the clearly positioned eye of a stable viewer, Neel's works seem to imagine a viewer who is mobile, constantly shifting the gaze they train on the painting. Neel further animates this unsteady gaze within the painting itself, in her curious portrayal of Buczak's eyes: it is as if his left eye is rendered higher on his face than his right eye. It also appears that Neel worked on Buczak's left eye at least twice; an overlayer of blue outline creates an uncanny effect in his gaze. Buczak looks up from the book, staring back at the viewer, and ostensibly at Neel as she created the painting. His own vantage point thus comes to the fore: From

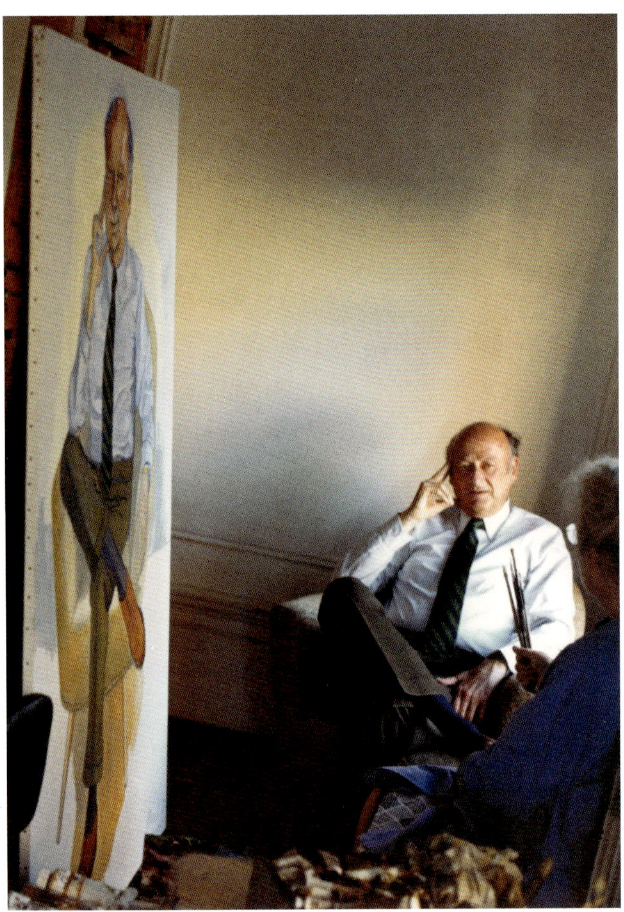

Mayor Ed Koch posing for a portrait by Alice Neel, c. 1981

what position and point of view does Buczak see, and what does the world look like through his eyes?

Like Neel, Buczak was a painter, producing about four hundred paintings and hundreds of drawings as well as artist books, performances, and more, in just over a decade of prolific creative production.[3] Buczak himself noted that he was in part "trying to paint the abstract, the idea of the spirit, the psyche, the soul."[4] Brad Melamed, an artist and Buczak's friend, wrote of his art: "Employing a variety of painting styles, he reinterprets childhood textbook illustrations, 19th century academic painting, biology, pornography, advertising, news media and other found imagery, creating a symbolic iconography that in his words was a 'search for accidental significance.'"[5] In Jasper Johnsian fashion, Buczak created many paintings of American flags—for example, *Flags I* (1986; p. 135), in which he depicts a group of about a dozen American flags against a sky-blue background, their proliferation both fervid and disquieting. Buczak's *Flags* paintings take on a tragic irony given that he passed from AIDS-related complications on July 4, 1987.

Buczak's affiliations and networks provide a sense of the connections and bonds central to his life and artistic practice. *Flags I* was selected by Felix Gonzalez-Torres for the cover of the 1990 New Museum publication *Out There: Marginalization and Contemporary Cultures*, which anthologized essays by Douglas Crimp, Audre Lorde, Kobena Mercer, Michele Wallace, Simon Watney, Cornel West, and other influential thinkers from that adamant moment of activist cultural production and theoretical discourse. Another version of *Flags* also graces the cover of *The Search for Accidental Significance: For Brian Buczak*, the 1987 memorial publication dedicated to Buczak after his death, edited by his partner, the artist Geoffrey Hendricks, with Melamed and artist Andrea Evans. The memorial tribute brings together Buczak's creative communities in book form, as more than one hundred friends and fellow artists contributed artworks and words to the heartfelt publication, including George Brecht, Simone Forti, Leon Golub, Ray Johnson, Joan Jonas, Taylor Mead, Barbara and Peter Moore, Nam June Paik, Carolee Schneemann, Nancy Spero, and Lawrence Weiner.[6] Louise Bourgeois dedicated her drawing "To Brian, the man with the beautiful liberating laugh."[7]

Brian Buczak witnessed the AIDS pandemic from within the artistic and queer communities devastated by it, and experienced AIDS with the intimacy of his own body. New York City mayor Ed Koch, a closeted gay man who helmed the governmental mismanagement of the AIDS crisis, occupied a vastly different position. Yet in Neel's painting *Mayor Koch* (1981; p. 125), created two years prior to *Brian Buczak*, Koch appears to be sitting in the same plush olive-brown chair as Buczak. Neel met Koch at a benefit dinner at Harold Reed Gallery in 1980, where her well-known nude self-portrait was first shown.[8] Koch "fell in love" with the work and agreed to be painted by Neel, though he did not agree to her suggestion that she paint him nude.[9] Still, Neel's portrait shows Koch jacketless, in relatively casual shirtsleeves and tie; recalling the sky in Buczak's *Flags* paintings, Neel's beautiful depiction of Koch's dress shirt is a swirl of sky-blue paint and small areas of blank canvas. Koch raises his right hand to his face in contemplation, with what Neel subsequently described as a "quizzical expression."[10] Sharp angles in both the position of Koch's oversized feet and the legs of the chair, as well as his bent knees and pointed collar, impart a staunch angularity to the painting. Though Neel paints a blue line on the right-hand side to differentiate floor from wall, it is on a different level and more or less disintegrates into a swatch of blue paint on the left portion of the painting, disrupting the figure-ground relationship. Untethered to a coherent picture plane, the chair in which Koch is seated appears slightly tilted. The portrait gives more of a sense of Koch's energy and aura than of his actual environment, highlighting Neel's propensity for the painterly.

In 1981, when Neel created her portrait of Koch, the first reports of what would become known as HIV/AIDS were influentially and infamously published in medical journals such as the *Morbidity and Mortality Weekly Report* and in popular press including *The New York Times*.[11] Though neither Koch nor Neel could have realized the extent to which AIDS had already begun working its way through New York City's population and beyond. Koch served as mayor for three terms, from 1978 to 1989, during which time the virus spread rampantly, with New York City as one of the pandemic's epicenters. While Koch signed a landmark executive order in his first year as mayor barring discrimination against homosexual people within the city government, his administrative policies toward AIDS were woefully negligent. In a 2022 *New York Times* article by Matt Flegenheimer and Rosa Goldensohn that outed Koch as a closeted gay man—almost a decade after his death in 2013—the authors contextualized the mayor's AIDS-related foundering: "The city's first comprehensive AIDS plan was not issued until 1988. Pleas for increased funding and the full use of the executive bully pulpit often went unheeded, a reticence that advocates found especially maddening."[12] In response, AIDS activists frequently targeted Koch, with Larry Kramer most vociferous among them in his attempts to publicly out Koch and incite greater accountability and action around AIDS. A particularly pointed AIDS

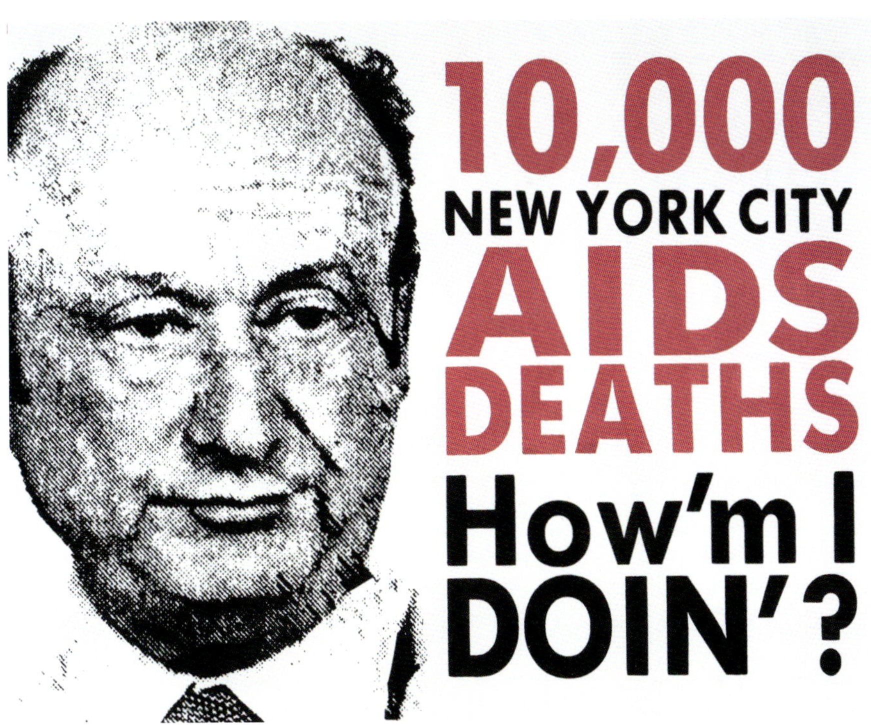

ACT UP New York, *10,000 New York City AIDS Deaths. How'm I Doin'?*, poster, 1989. Created by Richard Deagle for ACT UP's Target City Hall demonstration, 1989

activist demonstration poster pictured Koch staring grimly, with stark text in red and black reading: "10,000 NEW YORK CITY AIDS DEATHS. How'm I DOIN'?" Referencing Koch's characteristic political catchphrase, the poster critiqued Koch's record on AIDS and framed his complicity in the mounting maelstrom of AIDS-related deaths.

While sitting for Neel, might Koch have asked her, "How'm I doin'?" While with Neel during their session, did Buczak crack his "liberating laugh"? Neel's horizontal, sidelong painting of Buczak in repose, shirt open to mid-chest, contrasts with the verticality and frontality of her depiction of the more uptight Koch, his necktie tightly fastened. Yet despite their differences, Buczak and Koch both appear with legs crossed in a rather fey posture, apparently in the same chair. We can imagine them both sitting for Neel in this chair in her apartment as she painted their portraits, which record this proximity across time and space.[13] Indeed, this brief connection of their paths in Neel's home offers us a window onto the ways in which these two paintings point to the contrasts and convergences between the bohemian Buczak and the closeted politician Koch, both gay men in New York City, both painted by Neel in the final years of her life. All told, the AIDS pandemic deeply impacted the lives of Buczak and Koch, as it did and continues to for generations of New Yorkers, queer people, women, people of color, and so many more—everyone, all of us, really.[14] While portraiture may privilege the discrete individual, considering the vantage points of the sitters in Neel's paintings situates them in relation to one another and to their shared history through their differences—openness and denial, vulnerability and power—and their inextricable links.

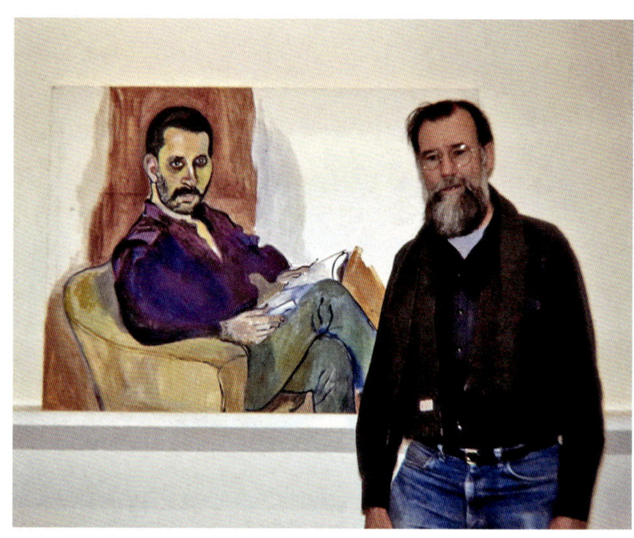

Geoffrey Hendricks with Alice Neel's *Brian Buczak* (1983), 1988

Notes

I am grateful to Andrea Evans, Brad Melamed, and Geoffrey Hendricks's longtime partner Sur Rodney (Sur), for their support of this essay, as well as their long-standing commitment to stewarding Brian Buczak's and Geoffrey Hendricks's art and legacies. I am also grateful to Elizabeth Keto, for her thoughtful edit and suggestions for this writing.

1 Randall Griffey, "Painting Fruit(s)," in Kelly Baum and Randall Griffey, *Alice Neel: People Come First*. Exh. cat. (New York: The Metropolitan Museum of Art, 2021), p. 100.

2 Neel's first depiction of Buczak was in the 1978 double portrait *Geoffrey Hendricks and Brian* (p. 112), which pictures Buczak in a loving embrace with his decade-long partner, artist Geoffrey Hendricks. A mainstay of Fluxus and happenings who taught for nearly fifty years at Rutgers University, Hendricks recalled of Neel: "While she was painting, her focus was totally on the painting. We had to sit without moving until she said we could take a break. It was not a conversational situation at all—that came before and after." Johnny Misheff, "Visiting Artists: Geoffrey Hendricks," *T: The New York Times Style Magazine* (May 15, 2012), accessed online.

3 Buczak's friends and fellow artists Andrea Evans and Brad Melamed provided these details of his creative output. Email correspondence with the author, August 3, 2023.

4 *Brian Buczak: A Memorial Exhibition*. Exh. cat. (New York: Money for Food, 1989), n.p.

5 Brad Melamed, text commissioned and adapted for the press release of *Brian Buczak: Man Looks at the World*, Ortuzar Projects, New York, 2024, p. 1.

6 Geoffrey Hendricks, Andrea Evans, and Brad Melamed, *The Search for Accidental Significance: For Brian Buczak* (New York: Money for Food, 1987). Two other texts in Buczak's memorial publication point to the realities of medical affliction and mourning in the context of AIDS. In a letter addressed to Larry Miller and Sara Seagull, reproduced as their contribution to the memorial publication, Buczak himself writes, "Dear Larry + Sara, Thanks for the card and the caring and concern. I'm hooked up to a blood pressure machine on one arm, oxygen in my mouth, an IV in my shoulder but that's nothing compared to when I first got in here collapsed lung, tube down my nose, tube in my side and I have AIDS. So I'm all set to go off to the other side, the spirit world, the whole deal white peace tranquility love John Lennon, Gustav Mahler Pope Paul I Duchamp Cornell George all my buddies." And Buczak's partner Geoffrey Hendricks writes in his "Elegy for Brian Buczak": "The night before last I talked with a friend about another friend's battle with AIDS, and in the depth of my grief realized that the understanding I gained from the experiences of my grief is there to be used to help others see and do what needs to be done." Hendricks would go on to be a steadfast supporter of the AIDS awareness arts organization Visual AIDS, actively involved in stewarding many of the organization's foundational programs including The Archive Project and serving on the board of directors for more than a decade. It is through my own involvement with Visual AIDS, where I worked as programs director from 2014 to 2019, that I met Hendricks and first learned of Buczak's art, life, and legacy.

7 *The Search for Accidental Significance*, n.p.

8 Phoebe Hoban, *Alice Neel: The Art of Not Sitting Pretty* (New York: David Zwirner Books, 2021), p. 371. First published 2010 by St. Martin's Press.

9 Hoban, *Alice Neel*, p. 374.

10 Hoban, *Alice Neel*, p. 384.

11 Michael Gottlieb, "Pneumocystis Pneumonia—Los Angeles," *Morbidity and Mortality Weekly Report* (June 5, 1981), pp. 250–252; Lawrence K. Altman, "Rare Cancer Seen in 41 Homosexuals," *The New York Times* (July 3, 1981), p. A20.

12 Matt Flegenheimer and Rosa Goldensohn, "The Secrets Ed Koch Carried," *The New York Times* (May 8, 2022), p. A1.

13 Neel's biography points to the location in which Neel painted Koch, noting that "the mayor . . . posed at Neel's apartment." Hoban, p. 387.

14 By the early 1990s, the word "queer," originally a derogatory term, was reclaimed by AIDS activists in collectives such as Queer Nation and academics with intellectual formations such as queer theory, and was eventually embraced as an umbrella term by and for LGBTQIA+ people.

LIST OF WORKS

Adrienne Rich, 1973
Ink on paper
29 ¾ × 22 inches
75.6 × 55.9 cm
Collection of Doug Woodham and Dalya Inhaber
p. 96

Al Freer, 1946
Oil on canvas
32 × 22 inches
81.3 × 55.9 cm
The Estate of Alice Neel
pp. 19, 20

Allen Ginsberg, 1966
Oil on canvas
50 × 35 ¼ inches
127 × 89.5 cm
The Estate of Alice Neel
p. 33

Andy Warhol, c. 1970
Ink, graphite, and gouache on tracing paper mounted on paper
6 ⅛ × 4 ¼ inches
15.6 × 10.8 cm
Collection of Valerie Carberry and Richard Wright, Chicago
p. 55

Annie Sprinkle, 1982
Oil on canvas
60 ⅞ × 44 ⅛ inches
154.6 × 112.1 cm
Private collection
p. 122

Arthur Bullowa, c. 1960
Oil on canvas
40 × 27 inches
101.6 × 68.6 cm
The Estate of Alice Neel
p. 41

Ballet Dancer, 1950
Oil on canvas
20 ⅛ × 42 ⅛ inches
51.1 × 107 cm
Hall Collection
pp. 26–27

Bella Abzug, 1976
Oil on canvas
108 × 60 inches
274.3 × 152.4 cm
Rowan University Art Gallery, Glassboro, New Jersey. Anonymous gift
p. 102

Brian Buczak, 1983
Oil on canvas
36 × 48 inches
91.4 × 121.9 cm
The Estate of Alice Neel
pp. 130–131

Christopher Lazare, 1932
Watercolor and collage on paper
12 ⅜ × 9 ¼ inches
31.4 × 23.5 cm
The Estate of Alice Neel
p. 15

Cuchulain, 1979
Oil on canvas
42 × 32 inches
106.7 × 81.3 cm
The Estate of Alice Neel
p. 115

David and Catherine Saalfield, 1982
Oil on canvas
55 × 40 inches
139.7 × 101.6 cm
Private collection, New York
p. 128

Dennis Florio, 1978
Oil on canvas
48 × 38 inches
121.9 × 96.5 cm
Private collection, Hong Kong
p. 110

Frank O'Hara No. 2, 1960
Oil on canvas
38 × 24 inches
96.5 × 61 cm
The Estate of Alice Neel
p. 29

Geoffrey Hendricks and Brian, 1978
Oil on canvas
44 × 34 inches
111.8 × 86.4 cm
San Francisco Museum of Modern Art. Purchase, by exchange, through an anonymous gift
p. 112

Gerard Malanga, 1969
Oil on canvas
60 × 40 inches
152.4 × 101.6 cm
Private collection
p. 62

Henry Geldzahler, 1967
Oil on canvas
50 × 33 ⅞ inches
127 × 86 cm
The Metropolitan Museum of Art, New York. Anonymous gift, 1981
p. 46

Jackie Curtis and Ritta Redd, 1970
Oil on canvas
60 × 41 ⅞ inches
152.4 × 106.4 cm
Cleveland Museum of Art. Leonard C. Hanna, Jr. Fund
pp. 57, 58–59

Jackie Curtis as a Boy, 1972
Oil on canvas
44 × 30 inches
111.8 × 76.2 cm
The Estate of Alice Neel
p. 99

John Cheim, 1979
Oil on canvas
45 ½ × 30 inches
115.6 × 76.2 cm
The Estate of Alice Neel
p. 117

Kate Millett, 1970
Oil on canvas
39 ¾ × 28 ½ inches
101 × 72.4 cm
National Portrait Gallery, Smithsonian Institution, Washington, DC. Gift of *Time* magazine
p. 52

Kris Kirsten, 1971
Oil on canvas
47 ⅞ × 30 inches
121.6 × 76.2 cm
The Estate of Alice Neel
p. 93

Martin Jay, 1932
Oil on canvas
25 × 20 ¼ inches
63.5 × 51.4 cm
The Estate of Alice Neel
p. 13

Marxist Girl (Irene Peslikis), 1972
Oil on canvas
60 × 40 inches
152.4 × 101.6 cm
Collection of Daryl and Steven Roth
pp. 88, 90–91

Mary D. Garrard, 1977
Oil on canvas
33 ¼ × 29 ¼ inches
84.5 × 74.3 cm
Private collection
p. 107

Mary Garrard, 1977
Ink and graphite on paper
30 ⅛ × 22 ½ inches
76.5 × 57.1 cm
The Estate of Alice Neel
p. 109

Max White, 1935
Oil on canvas
36 × 26 inches
91.4 × 66 cm
Smithsonian American Art Museum, Washington, DC. Museum purchase
p. 16

Mayor Koch, 1981
Oil on canvas
65 ¾ × 40 inches
167 × 101.6 cm
The Estate of Alice Neel
p. 125

Paul Kuyer, 1959
Oil on canvas
36 × 22 inches
91.4 × 55.9 cm
The Estate of Alice Neel
p. 22

Paul Kuyer, 1959
Oil on canvas
34 × 20 1/8 inches
86.4 × 51.1 cm
The Estate of Alice Neel
p. 24

Portrait of William D. Paul Jr., 1975
Oil on canvas
60 × 40 inches
152.4 × 101.6 cm
Georgia Museum of Art, University of Georgia, Athens. Gift of Richard, the artist's son, and Nancy Neel
p. 101

Richard Gibbs, 1961
Oil on canvas
25 × 16 inches
63.5 × 40.6 cm
Private collection, Australia
p. 36

Richard Gibbs, 1965
Oil on canvas
38 × 34 inches
96.5 × 86.4 cm
Private collection
p. 34

Richard Gibbs, 1968
Oil on canvas
64 × 50 inches
162.6 × 127 cm
Private collection, Minneapolis
p. 64

Richard Gibbs' Friend, c. 1962
Oil on canvas
42 × 31 inches
106.7 × 78.7 cm
The Estate of Alice Neel
p. 38

Robbie Tillotson, 1973
Oil on canvas
58 × 38 1/8 inches
147.3 × 96.8 cm
The Museum of Contemporary Art, Los Angeles. Gift of Hartley and Richard Neel
p. 94

Robert Avedis Hagopian, 1971
Oil on canvas
46 × 29 3/4 inches
116.8 × 75.6 cm
Fine Arts Museums of San Francisco. Gift of Richard H. and Beatrice Hagopian in memory of their son, Robert
p. 69

Ron Kajiwara, 1971
Oil on canvas
67 7/8 × 35 1/8 inches
172.4 × 89.2 cm
Alkar Contemporary Collection (ACC), Bilbao
p. 87

Rose Fried's Nephew, 1963
Oil on canvas
38 × 24 inches
96.5 × 61 cm
Wadsworth Atheneum Museum of Art, Hartford, Connecticut. The Ella Gallup Sumner and Mary Catlin Sumner Collection Fund. Dedicated to Susan A. Rottner in gratitude for her devoted service as President of the Wadsworth Atheneum Museum of Art Board of Trustees (2008–2011)
p. 49

Virgil Thomson, 1971
Oil on canvas
47 1/2 × 36 1/2 inches
120.7 × 92.7 cm
National Portrait Gallery, Smithsonian Institution, Washington, DC
p. 66

William Walton, 1967
Oil on canvas
48 × 33 inches
121.9 × 83.8 cm
National Gallery of Art, Washington, DC. Gift of Hartley S. Neel and Richard Neel
pp. 43, 44–45

CONTRIBUTORS

HILTON ALS is a journalist, critic, and curator. He has been a staff writer at *The New Yorker* since 1994. He has received numerous awards for his work, including the Pulitzer Prize for Criticism (2017), Yale's Windham-Campbell Literature Prize (2016), and a Guggenheim Fellowship (2000). His first book, *The Women*, was published in 1996. His book *White Girls* (2013) was a finalist for the National Book Critics Circle Award and the winner of the Lambda Literary Award in 2014. His most recent book, *My Pinup*, was published in 2022. He has curated critically lauded exhibitions, including *Alice Neel, Uptown*, David Zwirner, New York, and Victoria Miro, London (2017); *God Made My Face: A Collective Portrait of James Baldwin*, David Zwirner, New York (2019); and *Joan Didion: What She Means*, Hammer Museum, Los Angeles (2022), and Pérez Art Museum Miami (2023). He is currently a teaching professor at the University of California, Berkeley, and has also taught at Columbia University's School of the Arts, Princeton University, Wesleyan University, and the Yale School of Drama.

ALEX FIALHO is an art historian, curator, and PhD candidate in Yale University's combined PhD program in the history of art and African American studies. Fialho facilitated projects around the history and immediacy of the ongoing AIDS pandemic as programs director of the New York–based arts nonprofit Visual AIDS from 2014 to 2019 and conducted in-depth oral histories with fifteen cultural producers for the Smithsonian Archives of American Art's Visual Arts and the AIDS Epidemic: An Oral History Project. Fialho's writing has been published in exhibition catalogues for the Whitney Museum of American Art, Studio Museum in Harlem, Socrates Sculpture Park, and The Andy Warhol Museum, among other institutions. Fialho is a Helena Rubinstein Critical Studies Fellow in the Whitney Museum Independent Study Program (2023–2024).

EVAN GARZA is a curator, scholar, and a curatorial exchange initiative fellow at MASS MoCA in North Adams, Massachusetts. They were the 2021–2022 Fulbright US scholar at the Irish Museum of Modern Art (IMMA) in Dublin and a visiting research fellow in the Department of History of Art and Architecture at Trinity College Dublin. Garza, with Ryan N. Dennis, was an artistic director and curator of *A New Landscape, A Possible Horizon*, the 2021 Texas Biennial. In 2011 Garza was cofounder of Fire Island Artist Residency (FIAR), the first residency program exclusively for LGBTQ+ artists. Their writing on the work of global contemporary artists has been published by IMMA, The Drawing Center, *Flash Art*, *Art Papers*, *Hyperallergic*, and *Artforum*. Garza recently earned their MA in the Williams Graduate Program in the History of Art.

WAYNE KOESTENBAUM—poet, critic, fiction writer, artist, filmmaker—has published more than twenty books, including *Ultramarine* (2022), *The Cheerful Scapegoat* (2021), *Figure It Out* (2020), *Camp Marmalade* (2018), *Humiliation* (2011), *Hotel Theory* (2007), and *The Queen's Throat* (1993), which was nominated for a National Book Critics Circle Award. Recipient of a Guggenheim Fellowship in poetry, an American Academy of Arts and Letters Award in literature, and the Whiting Award, he is a distinguished professor of English, French, and comparative literature at the CUNY Graduate Center, New York.

ACKNOWLEDGMENTS

David Zwirner wishes to thank The Estate of Alice Neel, without whom this exhibition and catalogue would not have been possible, with special thanks to Ginny Neel for her invaluable contributions. Thanks are also due to Bellatrix Hubert for her close collaboration and support.

We are ever grateful to curator Hilton Als for his transformative engagement with Neel's work. Through his expansive and essential vision we experience Neel's work anew and in the broader context of its own time.

For their inspired and insightful texts, which so enrich our understanding of Alice Neel and the people she painted, we thank Alex Fialho, Evan Garza, and Wayne Koestenbaum.

The gallery would also like to specially acknowledge the institutional and private lenders who loaned works from their collections for the exhibition.

Thank you to everyone at David Zwirner who contributed to the exhibition, especially Rebecca Holmberg and Alexandra Whitney, as well as Melissa Acosta Morales, Rebecca Ashby-Colón, Claire Borre, Elizabeth Brannan-Williams, Allison Chipak, Joanna Fiorentino, Emily Gachot, Elizabeth Gartner, Brent Harada, Maris Hutchinson, Sophie Jenkins, Julia Lukacher, Kerry McFate, Ben McMillan, Britta Nelson, Kathryn Pinto, Harper Scott, and Virginia Stroh.

For the design of this catalogue, we extend our appreciation to Elizabeth Karp-Evans and Adam Turnbull of Pacific. For their help with its preparation, thanks are furthermore due to Sergio Brunelli, Luke Chase, Anna Drozda, Fabio Ferrandini, Doro Globus, Jessica Palinski Hoos, Daniela Ioan, Camilla Keil, Ayline Le Sourd, Mari Perina, Molly Stein, Jules Thomson, Anne Wehr, Maria Ylvisaker, Joey Young, and Lucas Zwirner.

Published by David Zwirner Books on the occasion of

At Home: Alice Neel in the Queer World
David Zwirner, 612 North Western Avenue, Los Angeles

Curated by Hilton Als

David Zwirner Books
520 West 20th Street, 2nd Floor
New York, New York 10011
+1 212 727 2070
davidzwirnerbooks.com

Editor: Anne Wehr
Editorial coordinator: Jessica Palinski Hoos
Proofreader: Anna Drozda

Design: Pacific
Photography coordination: Rebecca Ashby-Colón, Allison Chipak, Virginia Stroh
Production: Luke Chase, Jules Thomson
Color separations: VeronaLibri, Verona
Printer: VeronaLibri, Verona

Typefaces: GT Super DS, Kalice
Paper: Périgord, 170 gsm

Photography
Great care has been taken to credit all images correctly. In cases of errors or omissions, please contact the publisher so that corrections can be made in future editions.

Cover, p. 122: Photos by Kerry McFate; pp. 13, 19, 20, 24, 29, 33, 38, 41, 93, 99, 115, 117, back cover: Photos by Maris Hutchinson; p. 15: Photo by Ethan Palmer; p. 16: Photo courtesy Smithsonian American Art Museum, Washington, DC; pp. 22, 30, 34, 36, 52, 57, 58–59, 61, 69, 88, 90–91, 105, 112, 127, 128, 136: Photos courtesy The Estate of Alice Neel; pp. 26–27, 87: Photos by Dan Bradica; p. 31: Artwork © John Cohen Trust, courtesy L. Parker Stephenson Photographs, New York; pp. 43, 44–45: Photos courtesy National Gallery of Art, Washington, DC; p. 46: Image © The Metropolitan Museum of Art, New York; p. 49: Photo by Allen Phillips/Wadsworth Atheneum, Hartford, Connecticut; p. 50: Artwork © 2024 Jim Hubbard; pp. 51, 82: Photos by Fred W. McDarrah/Premium Collection via Getty Images; p. 55: Photo by James Prinz Photography; p. 62: Photo by Ove Kvavik/Munchmuseet, Oslo; p. 64: Photo by Malcolm Varon, New York; p. 66: Photo courtesy National Portrait Gallery, Smithsonian Institution, Washington, DC; p. 72: Artwork © 2023 The Peter Hujar Archive/Artists Rights Society (ARS), New York. Photo courtesy Pace, New York; p. 79: Photo © 2024 Daniel Nicoletta; p. 94: Photo by Brian Forrest; p. 96: Photo by Bruce White; p. 101: Photo by Michael McKelvey, 1998; p. 102: Photo by Karen Mauch Photography; p. 104: Photo courtesy Marjorie Kramer; p. 107: Photo by Greg Staley; p. 109: Photo by Adam Reich; p. 110: Photo © 2024 Christie's Images Limited; pp. 125, 130–131: Photos by Stephen Arnold; pp. 133, 138: Photos courtesy the Geoffrey Hendricks Estate; p. 135: Artwork © 2024 Brian Buczak. Photo courtesy the Geoffrey Hendricks Estate; p. 137: Photo courtesy ACT UP New York, Manuscripts and Archives Division, The New York Public Library

ISBN 978-1-64423-130-2

Library of Congress Control Number: 2023951665

Printed in Italy

Cover: *Annie Sprinkle*, 1982
Back cover: *Frank O'Hara No. 2*, 1960

Not all works in this publication were included in the exhibition at David Zwirner, Los Angeles. A checklist of the exhibition is available online at davidzwirner.com.